Nonverbal Messages:
Cracking the Code
My Life's Pursuit

by **Paul Ekman, PhD**

How a Behavior Scientist...

- Discovered that micro facial expressions reveal concealed emotions

- Proved that Darwin was right and Margaret Mead wrong about universals

- Escaped death (from a fellow scientist) while working in a Stone Age culture in New Guinea

- Invented the Facial Action Coding System (FACS), the first tool for measuring facial movements, later used by Pixar and Disney

- Discovered that making faces can turn on emotions

- Became buddies with the Dalai Lama, co-authoring a book together

- Worked as a saint buster for the Vatican

- Helped to get dissidents out of the Soviet Union

- Mapped the world of emotion for "navigators" to explore, creating with his daughter, Dr. Eve Ekman, an Atlas of Emotions

Nonverbal Messages:
Cracking the Code
My Life's Pursuit

Looking Behind the Curtain on How a Scientist Made His Discoveries

by **Dr. Paul Ekman**

Professor Emeritus, University of California, San Francisco
Founder, Paul Ekman Group LLC

Paul Ekman, Ph.D.
PO Box 26089
San Francisco, CA 94126-0689
Or email info@paulekman.com

ISBN: 978-0-9915636-3-0 pbk
       978-0-9915636-5-4 ebook

Cover and Interior Design:
Maureen Forys, Happenstance Type-O-Rama
Cover Photo: © 2016 Kingmond Young
Manufactured in the United States of America

Excerpt from *Believing Is Seeing: Observations on the Mysteries of
Photography,* by Errol Morris (New York: Penguin Press, 2011),
used by permission.

Cover Photos (clockwise from top)—*Backpacking in the Sierras
(1958)* • *Army basic training (1959)* • *Trip to Rome (1960)* • *Office in
San Francisco (1967 & 1969)* • *Wedding day (1979)* • *With Mary Ann;
Eve, at a few months old; and Tom, age eight (1980).*

First Edition
10 9 8 7 6 5 4 3 2 1

I dedicate this book to the people who took an interest in me when there was little certainty I would be worth it: Robert Berryman, Jerome Frank, Robert E. Harris, and Margaret Tresselt.

And to my family: Mary Ann, Eve, and Tom

Table of Contents

Introduction

WHAT MOTIVATED ME to spend fifty years investigating facial expressions, gestures, emotions, and lies? Why these topics, which had been abandoned as fruitless by the academic establishment? The early years of my life shaped who I am and what I chose to study, so I must start near the beginning as I seek to understand why I chose this particular focus to make my life's pursuit.

In much of my life I have been a bit oppositional, some would say rebellious, so I am not surprised that I gravitated towards topics scorned by academia as the stamping grounds of charlatans and fools. My eyes told me they were wrong. I delighted in the opportunity to prove that. But from where did my oppositional nature come, and the motivation that drove me unmercifully?

My first three school years were in Bragaw Avenue grammar school in Newark, New Jersey, in the late 1930s. (I was a year ahead of the noted novelist Phillip Roth. Unfortunately, we never met; students were strictly age-graded in those years.) In the second grade I scored the highest IQ recorded that year in New Jersey. I wasn't certain what that meant, but I did note that my parents were surprised. My older sister Joyce was supposed to be the smart one, not me, and certainly she was always a high academic achiever. A refrain repeated by most of my grammar school teachers: "I can't believe you are Joyce's brother. She was so well behaved, and such a good student!" My report cards alternated between A's and F's, and my behavior must not have been easy to deal with.

I have a vivid memory of behaving very aggressively—very. After a dispute with a neighboring boy (I wish I could remember what it was about), I went to the gardener's shed in our backyard, grabbed a hatchet, and chased him, threatening to cut his head off. Did I really do that? Did I really make that threat, or am I remembering an account I was told? My punishment was severe.

I was told I was going to jail, to pack some clothes in a small suitcase and wait (for what seemed like a few hours) for the police to take me away. My request to be allowed to write a letter to my kindergarten teacher, Mrs. Schaefer, whom I worshipped, was granted. Eventually a police car pulled up in front of our house. (I didn't know then that the police chief's child was my pediatrician father's patient—thus my father could enlist the police in his cruel charade.) After teary farewells to my mother and sister I entered the police car and was driven off. During a pause in the sobs I tried but failed to control, the police chief said I would be given another chance if I never again tried to hurt another boy. A promise I quickly granted.

Thirteen years later my father again tried to get me arrested. I was eighteen this time. I needed money for tuition to complete the last year of my undergraduate education. I told my father that the draft board had said that if I was out of school, even for one semester (time I would need if I had to earn the tuition money myself), they would immediately draft me to meet their quota for the Korean War.

Angry that I had not studied pre-med while at the University of Chicago, and not understanding that there were no electives for undergraduates at the U. of C. at that time, my father felt betrayed. Even worse, I wanted to become a psychologist! He had contempt for psychiatry, even more for psychology, an attitude frequently visited on my mother in the year before her suicide when she was receiving psychiatric treatment. When my father refused to give me the money unless I lived at home "under his thumb" as he put it, I asked him if we couldn't break the chain. I knew his father, my grandfather, had not allowed him to go to high school because his older brother didn't want to go, and my grandfather believed the younger brother should not exceed the older brother. So, at the age of twelve my father had to leave home and work his way through high school, college, and medical school. I knew he hated and resented his father.

After my request to break the chain, I asked my father if he wanted me to hate him like he hated his father. He knocked me to the floor. (My father had been a very good boxer in college, but he didn't need any special skill to get in this blow, as I was not expecting a fistfight.) When I got up I told him that I was now bigger than he was and if he ever hit me again I would hit him back. My father responded by calling the police chief and asking that I be arrested for threatening his life. I left home without waiting a minute, with only the clothes on my back and a few dollars in my pocket. I didn't see my father again for ten years.

In addition to being hit and threatened with jail, I had a second reason for hating my father. I held my father at least partially responsible for my mother's suicide. She took her life when I was fourteen. For the year preceding this desperate act, every evening at the dining room table my father would ridicule my mother for seeing a psychiatrist, bringing my mother to tears, again and again. The night before she killed herself she told me that my father had been unfaithful repeatedly, even during their honeymoon. My mother asked me to promise to never be unfaithful to my wife. After her death, her psychiatrist told me that my father had been sabotaging his efforts.

It was upsetting to write this last paragraph, even though the events I am writing about occurred nearly seventy years ago. The scars from a parent's suicide never completely heal. And the hatred I felt for my father, paradoxically, made me develop his worse traits—repeatedly easily angered, often inappropriately. As I will explain later, it is only in the last decade, in my close friendship with the Dalai Lama, that anger has receded in my life, though certainly not completely.

I should mention that my father was an excellent doctor, loved by his patients (sometimes inappropriately!). I remember him sitting at the kitchen table every night, reading the latest medical journals. He was a scholarly pediatrician. In the early 1950s, after a year of psychoanalytic therapy for severe migraines, I made two discoveries. First, I could succeed academically; I could use the intelligence I had inherited from my father without otherwise being him. Once I knew this on a gut level I became a straight-A student, an overachiever, disappointed that the exams I took were too easy, looking for challenges I could master. Second, I recognized that migraines occurred when I was, or thought I was, at the mercy of some arbitrary authority figure. I have managed in most of my adult life not to have a boss, for I could not easily cope with one.

My father enlisted in the army in 1942, although he was too old to have been drafted. Would he have done so if he wasn't Jewish? I never thought to ask him, as I had learned early not to disturb this unpredictable elephant. After a year of moving from one army base to another, changing schools three times that first year, we settled for the next three years in Pasadena, California, where a radical change in my approach to life was forced upon me. After a happy first two months attending John Marshal Junior High School, everything abruptly exploded. The band teacher (I played the clarinet, badly) asked each student to name the church he or she attended. When I said I was Jewish the teacher asked me to come to the front of the class and bend over so my fellow students could see my horns. I didn't know if I had them, but the looks of disappointment in my classmates' faces let me know that if I did, the horns must have been too small to be visible. The boy I regarded as my closest friend complained after class that I had ruined his reputation for having befriended a Christ killer. Those were the last words he spoke to me. They were the last words any child spoke to me for the next two and a half years.

Growing up in Newark, New Jersey, I had never encountered nor heard about anti-Semitism, as we lived in a heavily Jewish neighborhood. Anti-Semitism was very confusing to my nine-year-old mind. Hitler was killing the Jews, and my father had enlisted in the army to help in the war against him, yet some of the people in Pasadena wanted to kill us. Soon after I revealed we were Jewish in band class, there were bomb threats against our house, which brought out FBI protection for an army officer. My fellow students gave me the silent treatment for the next few years and threatened to beat me up (they did once), and so I was let out of school early every day. Between the ages of nine and twelve, I had no opportunity for friendship. Slowly I became resentful towards my fellow students, resentful towards my teachers. Resentful!

This is where I trace the origin of my oppositional, somewhat rebellious nature as an adolescent and as an adult. I was forced to become self-sufficient. I became my only friend. I began to talk to myself, encouraging myself in whatever I did, a habit I continue to this day, although now I do have friends. I am intolerant of anti-Semitism in any form, to which I respond with anger.

In that same period in Pasadena, my mother became mentally ill. She developed what would now be called bipolar disorder. Only I didn't know she was crazy. When she told me I was evil and would grow up to jump off a building, I believed her. She was my mother, the shining light in my life. It was only a few years later, after she failed in her first serious suicide attempt, that I realized she was not sane. I was fourteen when she asked me to save her the night before she successfully took her life. I couldn't;

I didn't know what to do. After her death I pledged to her and to myself that I would dedicate my life to helping people like her. I had no choice; I was obligated by my failure to save my mother from herself.

I was a driven, oppositional, resentful, increasingly angry, and very guilty adolescent. After the war we returned to New Jersey. When my homeroom teacher announced at the start of the ninth grade the authors whose works we would read, I asked "Why no Hemingway?" She replied, "Because I am the teacher." Impulsively, without consideration of what it would mean to challenge and insult a teacher in front of the class, I said "Why did we just fight a war against Hitler to have a dictator in the homeroom?" I was expelled for two weeks.

My admired history teacher, Mrs. McGaw, told me I had the audacity of a brass monkey. I found "audacity" in the dictionary, but it was a few months before I could find out what the phrase "brass monkey" implied. I liked it when I did. I have wanted to be that brass monkey and prove the world wrong. That is part of why I chose the topics of my research; it was an act of defiance. Expiating my guilt for failing to save my mother from her out-of-control emotions was an equally strong motivation for choosing what I have studied. Did I understand this before? No; only now as I write.

In my sophomore year of high school I learned from a friend that the College of the University of Chicago would admit you after two years of high school if you passed their entrance exam—an IQ test. This was the route I desperately needed to escape the rigidity of high school, my father's angry outbursts, and my knowledge of his ongoing dalliances, which did not stop for even a moment after my mother killed herself. He was delighted to have me go far away.

During the decades when the College of the University of Chicago was run by the educator Robert Hutchins, rebelliousness, unorthodoxy, and critical thinking were the flags students were expected to carry. "Challenge authority" was our motto before it became a bumper sticker. I loved it. The other unwritten guideline was "don't do anything unless you can do it superbly"—nothing but the best was acceptable. Aim high, as high as you can and get there! The array of talent among this college for misfits was amazing. To name just a few of my now best-known fellow students, Susan Sontag sat next to me in most of my classes, so shy she rarely uttered a word even though the teaching method was to use discussions, not lectures. And, Mike Nichols and Elaine May were a year ahead. It was a high standard, which I relished.

I chose two identity badges: photography and Freud. In junior high I had developed some talent as a self-taught photographer, which enabled me to become the self-appointed, but widely accepted, class photographer, chronicling the life of my fellow students. Freud I first encountered in a class on rhetoric. Splendid rhetoric it was, but it also promised to help me understand my mother's and my agonies. I became the class Freud expert/scholar, reading everything he had written that was available in English, so I could quote Freud at appropriate moments. I decided I would become a psychoanalyst—a lay, non-medical, analyst as Freud praised in his book *Lay Analysis*. This path allowed me to become a doctor without taking the medical route, avoiding my father's path. I had by then come to blame him, I now think unfairly, for my mother's suicide.

No psychology department, not even Chicago's, would accept an applicant for graduate school who did not have an undergraduate major in psychology. Since there were no major or minors in the undergraduate program at the University of Chicago I had to go elsewhere in order to major in psychology. The University of Minnesota accepted me, providing a major in psychology in one year. But, I didn't know anyone in Minneapolis, and having to support myself I instead went to NYU, where it took two years to get the psychology major I needed but I knew I could get a job to support myself.

(As I write this I just read the first report of how a father who has been traumatized will pass on in his genes the impact of that trauma to his offspring.[1] If that is really true, then there has been a long chain in my father's side of the family. Is there anyone to really blame for being abusive? Long before I read this article I believed I had to struggle to overcome my inheritance of impatience and hot anger. I believe that through my contact with the Dalai Lama a decade ago I finally did succeed at least partially in repairing my personality and emotion system. More about that much later.)

After fleeing my father's attempt to have me arrested I slept for a few nights on the couch in my sister's apartment. I went to see the draft board, telling them I would have to be out of school for one semester in order to earn tuition money. Without a student deferment, for even one semester, they said I would immediately be drafted to meet their quota for the Korean War. I asked my maternal uncles for help, and they rescued me with a gift of the first year's tuition. In a recent book I thanked them in the acknowledgments: "...to my maternal uncles, Leo Siegel and the late Robert Semer. When I was eighteen, untried, and for the first time on my own in the world, they enabled me to continue my education. *Sine qua non*." Thereafter I earned my tuition by working as a bellhop during the summers in New Jersey shore resorts.

My weekly living costs were met by working twenty hours a week as a night clerk in a liquor store on the New York waterfront. There was a brothel on one side of the liquor store and a loan shark on the other side, with the headquarters of the longshoreman's union across the street, a hangout for the Mafia. I soon learned that the previous night clerk had been shot in a robbery. But the Mafia took a liking to the "college kid," and the word was spread that no one bothers the kid, and no one did. The longshoremen adopted me, leaving off each week some of what they were stealing from the ships they unloaded—a tree of bananas, a carton of canned tuna, etc.

By the time I was nineteen (in 1953) I was living with a dancer in the heart of Greenwich Village, midway between the liquor store and NYU. I was feeling great—self-sufficient, living the bohemian life, and absorbing the New York City culture, above and underground. Unfortunately, most of the courses at NYU were boring.

There had been no lectures or textbooks at Chicago; instead we had discussions and original great books as sources. At NYU, after the teacher in the first class meeting on adolescent psychology lectured for an hour, I reminded her of the research that showed people learned more from reading than hearing. I asked her to mimeograph her lecture notes and hand them out. She did not comply. Despite doing quite well on her final exam she gave me a D.

Margaret Tresselt taught the experimental psychology class. I loved Tresselt's enthusiasm for learning from an experiment something we didn't already know. She invited students to hang out in her lab, and I volunteered for any task she could show me how to do. I didn't conceptualize it then, but I can see now that Tresselt conducted her research in order to explore, to find out something new, rather than to test a hypothesis that she was already relatively certain was correct. That's a path I have followed; excited more by discovery than proof. Tresselt or one of her more senior students taught me how to run the IBM card sorter, doing an "analysis of variance" using the sorter! What fun!

The final exam required that we each design an experiment. Earlier that year I had the chance to observe a group therapy session, and I became convinced that it was the future rather than individual psychotherapy, since you could help more people at once. I thought it might be useful if we could measure at the outset of therapy the group members' attitudes towards peers (their fellow patients) and authority figures (the group therapist). The project I proposed to meet Professor Tresselt's class requirement was to measure each person's "Group Image." My test very much resembled the then popular Thematic Apperception Test (TAT).

To validate my Group Image test I would need to measure how people behaved during group sessions. One hour observing a group therapy session convinced me that it was often not what participants said, but their gestures and facial expressions that mattered. I learned also that the behavioral measure popular at the time—Bales's Interaction Process Analysis—was more reliable when people were directly observed rather than from an audio recording, confirming my hunch that the nonverbal behavior was crucial. Fortunately, I soon forgot about my Group Image test and in graduate school focused instead on how to measure the nonverbal behaviors.

I applied to twenty-two clinical psychology graduate schools. No one told me that you had to conceal an ambition to become a therapist, claiming to want only a research career. I didn't lie and was rejected by twenty of the schools. City College of New York was the only school that offered me an interview. I was then offered admission to what was a very good program, but it was only a master's level, and after the trauma of all the rejection letters I instead chose Adelphi College, which was the only Ph.D. program that sought to train psychotherapists.

I had superb training in psychological testing, taught by part-time faculty who were renowned masters of the Rorschach, the Wechsler-Bellevue IQ Test, the Draw a Person Test, and the TAT. I very much enjoyed testing; I only learned later that no one paid much attention to the test reports. The IQ tests—the Wechsler and the Stanford Binet—were taken more seriously. I found them fascinating to administer and interpret, it wasn't the total score that mattered, but the range of different abilities they revealed. My first job as a psychologist, during my second year in graduate school, was to give Stanford Binet's at $25 each to all the students at the Little Red School House in Greenwich Village. What a kick! The kids were so smart. I even met Pete Seeger, who came in once a week to teach a class on the recorder.

During my second and third years I did individual psychotherapy, audio recording my sessions and receiving two hours of supervision, from two different supervisors, for every hour I saw a patient. It was amazing, enlightening, and sometimes very confusing training. I loved it. My supervisors praised my budding talents, encouraging me to pursue a career as a therapist. In my third year I had another part-time job at a private mental hospital, doing intake interviews. I also administered the initial neurological exams, having taken a very good yearlong course in clinical neurology. One adolescent girl, in a classically catatonic state—eyes closed, unable to stand, no sign of hearing anything said to her, and refusing food—had received shock treatments, which didn't help. She was not expected to survive the heat of the summer in the hospital ward, which had no air conditioning. Since the hospital doctors had given up, I was allowed to try a psychotherapeutic approach. Studying the most recent book on the treatment of schizophrenia by Arieti,[2] I talked to her for two hours every day. She showed no response for weeks and then she recovered, slowly at first, but within the next month had a complete remission. The hospital staff thought it was my intervention, as did I. Now I am less certain, but it did strengthen my commitment to becoming a psychotherapist.

And then there was research. The only researcher on the faculty was Robert Berryman, a Skinnerian who did conditioning studies on rats. He was very bright and funny, and he took me into his lab, and into his life. I was the only student who was interested in learning about research. I became his unpaid research assistant. I learned how he thought about problems and incorporated it into my interests in nonverbal behavior. He encouraged me to pursue vigorously the development of methods for measuring the elusive expressions and gestures. True to the Skinnerian tradition, rate measures—how often something occurred—became my focus, counting movements that appeared to be similar, with little concern for how they related to what the person or anyone else was saying.

Constrained by the Skinnerian orientation of my mentor Berryman, I made little progress in my research on nonverbal behaviors. I never considered what had motivated the behavior I counted, failing to group together behaviors that differed in appearance but served similar functions within the interaction. All of those considerations came later when I emerged from Berryman's influence.

Nonverbal Messages:
Cracking the Code
My Life's Pursuit

First Experiment, 1955

ROBERT BERRYMAN, my mentor at Adelphi College, encouraged me to stake out a claim on the nonverbal territory. My first published article in a scientific journal (a second-tier journal, which now I believe did not merit even that status) was published in 1957 entitled, "A Methodological Discussion of Nonverbal Behavior."[3] The first two sentences were the best part of the article:

> *The behavior of the organism in any interpersonal situation can be classified into three categories: verbal, vocal, and nonverbal. These three types of behavior can be distinguished in terms of their medium of expression, the manner in which they are perceived, their developmental sequence, and their communicative value.*

It is the only one of my articles I have never cited, nor has nearly anyone else. But it was a start.

I don't remember how much of the design of my first experiment was influenced by Berryman, though he certainly encouraged me and was enthusiastic. I don't think I would ever have considered the possibility that I might have a research career without Berryman. Notice that the list is growing of older people who took an interest in me, helping me along and never asking for credit: my two uncles, Tresselt, and now Berryman.

The first edition of my first book, *Emotion in the Human Face*,[4] was dedicated to Berryman, Tresselt, Gordon Derner (the head of the Ph.D. program at Adelphi and chairman of my doctoral dissertation committee), and Robert E. Harris, chief psychologist at Langley Porter in San Francisco, where I did my clinical internship. Because of Harris's interest in me, I was able to submit an application for a postdoctoral fellowship, which I received from the National Institute of Mental Health (NIMH) in 1961 for the next three years, launching my research career. They were all alive when my first book was first published in 1972, and I sent each of them an inscribed copy. None of them are alive today.

I sent a copy to my father, of course, hoping it would upset him since he had never published an article, let alone a book. I also visited Columbia High School, which l had left after two boring years for the University of Chicago in 1949. When the principal heard I was applying to Chicago, he told me that the letter he would write about me would ensure I would *not* be admitted. I gave him a copy of the book, let him know I had a Ph.D., and expressed my resentment over his attempt to block me. He claimed he always knew I had it in me.

The aim of my first experiment was to prove that non-verbal behavior was an accurate source of information by showing it revealed whether or not people were under stress. Writing that sentence I am amazed that in the

1950s proof was needed. Academia had dismissed non-verbal behaviors as meaningless, at best a home for stereotypes. Many clinicians held the opposite view; when I first received funding from NIMH, at least half of the reviewing committee consisted of clinicians.

I designed my first experiment to prove nonverbal behaviors differed when people were under stress or relieved from stress. The participants were my fellow graduate students who were stressed when Professor Gordon Derner, the head of the clinical psychology program, criticized them. If participants said they intended to pursue a life of research, I had instructed Derner to criticize them for not wanting to help people, hiding in the laboratory. If they said they intended to go into practice, he criticized them for wanting to make money. I told him to never let a student finish a sentence, always interrupting and disagreeing with whatever they said. He was good at it, seeming to enjoy going for the jugular. Even though the students knew it was a research study, they also knew that a senior professor had the unquestioned power to throw any student out, for whatever reason he chose. We knew that at least one, sometimes two, of the eight students in each class was booted out every year.

After five minutes of attacks and interruptions, which reduced every student to inarticulate groans, Derner was signaled, by me, to stop the attacks and start the praise, telling each student how well he or she had handled the onslaught. They seemed to eat it up, enormously relieved.

I had only my still camera to record their nonverbal behavior. With a roll of 35mm film limited to thirty-six exposures, I took a photograph every fifteen seconds, recording nine minutes of interaction—five minutes in the criticism portion, four minutes of the praise. I built a rig that put an audible mark on a simultaneous audio recording exactly when each photograph was taken.

Untrained observers when shown the photographs were able to identify which had been taken during the criticism and which during the praise periods. They were also able to accurately locate where in the conversation a photograph had been taken. In one fell swoop, this initial study in 1956 proved two different but related ideas, contradicting the accepted wisdom within the academic establishment. First, nonverbal behaviors do contain *accurate* information about an interpersonal relationship. Second, this information is available, understood by untrained, ordinary people viewing the behavior without slowed motion or any other special aid. The first point could have been true, but not the second, if the clues within the nonverbal behavior were similar to micro expressions (which weren't discovered for another fifteen years), not recognized by most people without their having received specialized training. If that had been the case, I would not have obtained evidence for the first proposition—accurate information.

If the information was there but not obvious to the untrained eye, I might have reached the wrong conclusion. If that were so, the people to whom I showed the photographs would not have been able to tell which had been taken during the criticism or praise phases of the interview. Would I have continued? I don't know. I strongly sensed that the nonverbal behaviors contained accurate information; I thought I could see it. But if others couldn't, would I have trusted my intuition, or would I have given up? I hope not. But fortunately, that was not the case.

The reader today might not realize how lucky I was. I had only studied the behavior of two people during those stressful interviews. What if one of them had been unexpressive? Some people are. What if the stress had not been strong enough to generate changes in behavior? What if the students who were stressed were good at concealing how they felt? What if the changes in behavior were not understood by untrained people, but required measuring the behavior itself? I had not yet developed any tools for directly measuring nonverbal behavior.

But enough what-ifs. It worked! Cautious, knowing that academia would be surprised by what I found, I did not publish the findings for another decade, not until I had the opportunity to repeat the procedure with additional people undergoing a stressful interview and new people evaluating their behavior.[5] As I edit what I have written about what I did nearly sixty years ago, I am still astonished that I had to *prove* that nonverbal behaviors are meaningful. It is so obvious; it was soon taken for granted. But then it flew in the face of academic blindness or prejudice about this behavioral domain. And that pleased me no end! I haven't regarded these findings as one of my major scientific contributions, although considering it now, it was a landmark. It brought back into the scientific realm the examination of facial expression and gesture. It proved there was a lot there to be further uncovered.

This then is my first scientific *accomplishment*:

NUMBER 1 I proved that nonverbal behaviors provide accurate information. And it is not obscure; most people can derive at least some of that information with no trouble.

It doesn't seem like much now, but in 1956 it was near revolutionary! When I finally published all of the findings in 1965, it started the field of what was then called nonverbal communication or body language.

This first research study also suggested a methodological distinction: sometimes one of the photographs caught an *act*—a movement of the hands, legs, or a facial expression. Sometimes the photograph recorded a static *position* of the entire face and body. Both contained information, in that the observers shown in the photographs were able to detect whether they were taken during stress or praise regardless of whether they revealed acts or positions. I was to focus my research on extracting the information from acts, failing to find a way to measure the information contained in positions. I described the distinction between acts and positions in an article published some years later.[6]

In my very first experiment I made an important discovery—*emblematic slips*, the gestural equivalents of slips of the tongue. I adopted the term "emblem" from David Efron,[7] a pioneer in the study of nonverbal behavior who had distinguished symbolic gestures, which he called emblems, from movements that accompanied speech, which I labeled *illustrators*. While most emblems are performed with as much awareness as are the words they repeat or for which they are a substitute, I discovered that emblematic slips occur without the person who shows it being aware that he or she is revealing information. My later cross-cultural research was to show that Darwin[8] was correct in his claim that emblems (he called them gestures, a term I avoid unless I wish to refer to the aggregate of emblems and illustrators) are culture-specific. My research on emblems is reported in other later articles.[9], [10], [11]

My fellow student, the late Rhoda Krawitz, was older than most of her fellow students and not accustomed to being treated as disrespectfully as she was by professor Derner during the stressful portion of the interview. Halfway through that assault, she gave him the finger, but with that finger resting on her lap, not up in the space in front of her, in what I subsequently called the *presentation position*, where emblems, if they are not slips, are usually shown. My research on deception twenty years later found many instances of emblematic slips, the most common one being a fragment of the shrug, contradicting the words as they are spoken.

I noticed this emblematic slip when it occurred, as I watched each interview through a one-way vision screen, operating my 35mm camera. Both Rhoda, who was to become one of my closest friends over the next nearly fifty years, and Derner denied what I claimed to have seen. But the film caught it. Rhoda was very aware of suppressing her anger at Derner for his mistreatment of her and wanted to give him the finger, but wasn't aware she had done so. I rejoiced in having seen something no one else had every reported seeing, a gestural equivalent of a slip of the tongue. I wanted more discoveries. They were to come, slowly but steadily, as I plowed untilled fields.

NUMBER 2 Gestural slips exist, which leak suppressed information. This was a discovery, not a proof like Number 1.

It still pleases me that I saw something no one had ever before reported seeing. A gestural slip is always just a fragment of the full gesture or emblem, to use the technical name, and it is always out of the presentation position. Since emblems are culture-specific, not universal, as Darwin had predicted, people are unlikely to recognize them when they are talking to someone from another culture. I have failed in repeated attempts to convince our government to map the vocabulary of emblems specific to the various countries, and there are many of them now, which may be a source of terrorist acts against us. To identify the emblem "vocabulary" for any ethnic group takes about four months of one person.

A few more words about David Efron. His book, published in 1941, compared East European Jews and Sicilian immigrants to the lower east side of New York and their offspring. The introduction was written by one of the most famous psychologists of that time, Gordon Allport, heralding the importance of Efron's research. Efron had been a student of the then-famous anthropologist Franz Boas at Columbia University. Boaz had urged his students to challenge the writings of the Nazi-influenced German social scientists during the 1930s, who claimed that gestures were genetically based markers that betrayed the origins of the inferior races, allowing the easy identification of Jews, Poles, and Gypsies. Efron proved that although the gestures of the immigrant Lithuanian Jews and Sicilian Italians he studied on the lower east side of Manhattan were remarkably different, those differences disappeared in their offspring who attended integrated schools.

The publication of Efron's book coincided with the U.S. entrance into World War II. Efron's great work was lost, rarely cited, until I discovered a summary of his findings in the first handbook of social psychology. Efron, an

Argentinean Jew, returned to Argentina and then took a job with the World Health Organization in Geneva. I found him. When we met, he suggested that we jointly repeat his research in Israel, but I failed to obtain support for such a study from any of the foundations that support anthropological research, and we lost touch. An Internet search reveals only his publication of the one book I mentioned, nothing about his subsequent career or the year of his death.

The three major influences on my thinking about nonverbal behaviors were Efron, Silvan Tomkins, and Charles Darwin. I got to know personally the first two men, Darwin only by spending months going through the archives of his materials both at Cambridge University and at his home, Downe House. Darwin saved every letter written to him and from him (his wife made copies of every letter he sent), and also his detailed instructions to publishers.

More about my intellectual fathers, Tomkins and Darwin, later. But let me note here that, though I was ashamed of my actual father for his cruelty and infidelities, I failed then to acknowledge that he was also a brilliant man and a very good pediatrician. I did spend much of my life bringing honor to my three intellectual father figures: Efron, Tomkins, and Darwin (for his neglected book on expression). A few close colleagues have suggested a fourth benevolent father figure, the Dalai Lama. But he and I regard each other as brothers.

By the end of my first year of graduate school I wrote an application to NIMH for a research grant to study nonverbal behavior during psychotherapy sessions. At that time there was no biographical form, so NIMH did not know they were reviewing a grant proposal written by a twenty-year-old graduate student. None of my professors had ever had a grant, so none knew it was inappropriate for a graduate student to apply for one. NIMH sent Dr. Jerome Frank from Johns Hopkins in Maryland up to Long Island to interview me at Adelphi. I knew Frank's writings; he was a famous psychotherapy researcher. He was a very kind man, praising me for having written such a thoughtful and, he said, important research proposal, but the rules did not allow giving a research *grant* to a graduate student. He said he would arrange for me to get a pre-doctoral research *fellowship*, which he did, that supported me to do research for the next two years. This was the beginning of what eventuated in more than forty years of support from NIMH: a postdoctoral fellowship a few years later, followed by a succession of research grants, and many Research Scientist Awards. More than forty years later I dedicated my book, *Emotions Revealed*, to the staff of NIMH that had supported me for so many years. The director of NIMH, whom I met a few years ago, told me no one had ever dedicated a book to NIMH.

Realizing I was making no progress in my study of nonverbal behaviors, Berryman told me it might well take a decade to crack this nut. He advised me to turn elsewhere for a doctoral dissertation. It was just a hurdle to jump, he said, so I must find a dissertation study that would allow me to jump quickly. Verplanck and Greenspoon[12] had just published experiments showing it was possible to use the same model that had been successful for conditioning rats and pigeons to change human behavior. Berryman told me to read their work and figure out the next step.

No one yet had tried to use *operant conditioning* to modify something as complex as an opinion, which is what I chose to do. I compared a nonverbal (head nod and smile) with a verbal ("good") reinforcement for changing the research subjects' opinions about capital punishment. I would read to them each of more than fifty statements about capital punishment, and record their answers to the first group of statements, noting whether they were pro, anti, or undecided. Then I tried to change their opinions by administering reinforcement (head nod and smile, or verbal statement "good"). I tried to make the pro become anti, the anti become pro, and move the undecided one way or the other. The nonverbal was a bit more effective than the verbal reinforcement, but only for those who were undecided. I have never published this study, not thinking much of it, but it took me only five weeks from start to finish! And, as I explain later, it got me my first job after my discharge from the army.

Poring through the library for books written about nonverbal behavior I found a very interesting one, long on ideas and short on experiments, by the Gestalt psychologist Werner Wolff, who had immigrated to the U.S., landing at Bard College, just before the Nazi onslaught. I bored Wolff with my account of my observations of how people behaved during the stress interviews, but he was very interested in my account of what I had observed working in a mental hospital. The patients were treated as children, punished with shock treatment for misbehavior. (I no longer think much of that observation.) As the organizer of the Inter-American Congress of Psychology, he invited me to give a presentation at their next meeting and covered all my expenses. It was very exciting to have such an opportunity, although I remember little about it other than my failure to seduce a number of luscious South American students who attended the meeting.

The last requirement for obtaining a Ph.D. in clinical psychology was a yearlong clinical internship. I applied to a half dozen premier programs and was accepted by all of them. In addition to the Inter-American Congress and A's in all my classes, I had a published article—I looked good. I chose the Langley Porter Neuropsychiatric Institute, part of the University of California Medical Center in San Francisco. I had seen San Francisco when I was ten, on a family vacation, and decided then it was where I wanted to live. Also Jurgen Ruesch, a psychiatrist at Langley Porter, had that year co-authored a book entitled *Nonverbal Communication*. I had written a review, praising the many interesting ideas but criticizing it for a total lack of data, or even examples, but decided not to try to publish it if I wanted to be accepted at Langley Porter. It took seven months of requests before Ruesch deigned to meet with a lowly graduate student, and then he was very condescending. I was to get to know him a bit in later years, and respected him for his foresight. And I recognized that his clinical tradition of the time did not require research to back up the presentation of interesting ideas.

I conducted no research during my internship, but I learned about the Minnesota Multiphasic Personality Inventory (MMPI) personality test, which in the hands of good clinicians was surprisingly accurate. I had not expected this, having been schooled in the tradition of the Rorschach and the Thematic Apperception Tests. I loved San Francisco and decided that I would spend my life there, and that geography, location, was more important than career opportunities. I spent my spare time increasing my skills in photography, developing a series of photographs of modern dancers, which even today I consider quite good. I planned to split my time between photography and clinical practice, but the army changed that. I was drafted and required to report for officer basic training at Fort Sam Houston, in San Antonio, Texas, on September 10th, 1958, just ten days after my Ph.D. was awarded. Graduate school, including the year's internship, had taken four years.

CHAPTER 2

The U.S. Army Changed the Direction of My Career, 1958–1960

MY ASSIGNMENT AFTER FORT SAM was to be staff psychologist, and soon thereafter chief psychologist at Fort Dix, New Jersey (an infantry basic training camp), as 1st Lt. Paul Ekman. There were no opportunities to do psychotherapy; the recruits had no time and the regular army knew it was career suicide to admit to any psychological problems. But I had amazing research opportunities, with forty thousand men divided among four training regiments coming through every eight weeks. I had access to demographic information and the recruits' scores on a few army tests before they arrived.

I did three applied studies, obtained my first grant from the Surgeon General, and ran the army's largest psychological research program at the time, with ten drafted enlisted men, including PFC Wallace Friesen. Wally had dropped out of graduate school at the University of Kansas, but had acquired a keen appreciation of the research process while working with Professor Paul Gump. I appointed Wally to be my research coordinator, and we became friends, although if he were to be heard to address me by my first name, he would have been court-martialed.

I was required on occasion to see a prisoner in the stockade, a prison surrounded by barbed wire with machine guns at each corner to deter escape. The crime that landed nearly all the recruits there was going AWOL—running away—an offense that does not exist in civilian life. I learned that most of the prisoners had turned themselves in, guilty about their failure to endure basic training. The standard punishment for a first AWOL offender was a month in the stockade. Remorse about having gone AWOL soon changed into defiance and anger at the army. Almost all of them went AWOL again the moment they got out, having discovered the unwritten rule: three AWOLs would be rewarded by a discharge, albeit a dishonorable discharge.

I convinced the Commanding General to allow me to do an experiment comparing a month in the stockade with three hours a day of extra hard labor but no imprisonment. I matched prisoners who were to receive each of the punishments by their IQ on the army's standard test, length of time before going AWOL, and how long they were AWOL before turning themselves in. A six-month follow-up showed an enormous difference in recidivism; much less for those who did not go into the stockade. On that basis, the General changed the punishment for first AWOLs; no longer did they get sent to the stockade. Research had changed the environment, making it more humane and more effective. I began to think that research was the way to benefit the world, much more than psycho-therapy could ever be.

My second study generated another major change in how the army treated recruits. Up until my research the army made it very difficult for a recruit to get to the Mental Health Clinic, fearing everyone might try to get a discharge. One of the unintended consequences of this barrier was that recruits who were having a panic attack were not diagnosed for nearly two months. Many then had a psychotic episode near the end of basic training and had to be hospitalized, often for a few months, before being discharged. I convinced the General to allow me to do another experiment. In two of the four training regiments I met with all the recruits in the first two days, telling them that if they were not man enough to make it, come to the clinic and we would give them a discharge (not a dishonorable one). In the other two training regiments the usual practice of preventing access to mental health service until late in training continued. As I expected, there was no difference in the discharge rate between the regiments in which there was access to mental health services in the first week and those where such access was blocked until late in training. But the number of recruits who had to be hospitalized dropped in the regiments where early access to mental health facilities was allowed. So, the General changed access to mental health facilities for all training regiments from there on. Once again research had changed the environment, this time reducing acute mental illness episodes.

I was convinced that research would now be my path, but I had not had much research training and knew that what I had learned from Berryman was not sufficient, and not appropriate to what I wanted to study. With encouragement from the head of psychology at Langley Porter, Robert E. Harris, who had taken an interest in me during my internship year, I applied to NIMH for a three-year postdoctoral research fellowship, which was awarded.

I did one more study that changed army practices showing that psychiatric assessment within a day of admission to the hospital was just as accurate as assessments done a week later (which had been the standard practice, waiting for the patient to "quiet down"). Earlier assessment meant earlier diagnosis, treatment, or discharge.

I have only published about half of my findings, and that has been so throughout my career. Getting an article written in the format acceptable to scientific journals and then going through the review is a real time killer. Often once I know the answer to the question, I would rather invest that time in attacking another question than publishing what I find. Sometimes someone else unwittingly repeats and publishes one of my many unpublished studies, but that never bothers me.

CHAPTER 3

First Full-Time Job and Postdoctoral Fellowship, 1961–1963

SHORTLY BEFORE I WAS DISCHARGED from the army, I was offered a research job at the Palo Alto VA, helping Leonard Krasner and Leonard Ullman in their grant-supported research using operant conditioning methods to treat psychiatric patients. I wanted the training offered by the postdoctoral fellowship at Langley Porter in San Francisco, but the VA position offered more than twice the salary, which would allow me to pay off the debts accumulated during graduate school and the army. I was allowed to postpone starting the fellowship for eleven months and took the VA job. I did not like the commute from San Francisco or the work, which entailed trying to replicate their earlier study that had shown the benefits of conditioning patients with mental health problems. It failed to replicate. It was no surprise to me, but a great disappointment to my employers. When I decided at that point to resign and take up the fellowship at Langley Porter, they were relieved, so we parted on friendly terms after three months, at the start of the New Year in 1961. I never checked to find out whether they published my failure to replicate, or even tried to replicate it again after I left.

The one highlight of my three months at the Palo Alto VA hospital was meeting the famous anthropologist Gregory Bateson. He took an interest in me, and we had many long conversations. Gregory was quite obscure but often illuminatingly brilliant. Gregory was quite taken with the Don Jackson group at the Mental Research Institute in Menlo Park, who were known at the time for writing about a "double bind" communication pattern responsible for the development of schizophrenia. Although he spent much of his time with the Jackson group, Gregory's salary was, for reasons I never understood, paid by the Palo Alto VA, where he played no role whatsoever, which seemed fine with him. Few people at the VA talked to him and the people I was working for at the VA had contempt for him, but I spent as much time with Gregory as I could.

He lent me the Leica camera he had used to do what I think may be the first photographic study of another culture—his photographic book on Bali published in the 1930s. He tried, without success, to convince me that emotion was the wrong framework for looking at facial expression, which should be communication instead. I knew he was wrong in seeing this as a choice, but I couldn't think it through clearly enough to explain why until many years after his death.

We lost contact when Gregory moved to the Oceanic Institute in Hawaii. I wrote him a few years later, saying that I was going to do field work in New Guinea. As I had hoped, he invited me to spend a few days with him and Lois, his then wife, on my way. We had a splendid few days. Gregory was studying a monkey who had free range of his house. Once again I understood only about half of what he told me about what he was learning. I knew he thought I was on the wrong track by relating facial movements to emotion not communication, but he gave me his blessing.

It was many years later before I could understand the matter well enough to explain why emotion and communication were both relevant to understanding facial expressions. I quote here from what I wrote as if I were talking to Gregory in the afterword of the third edition of Darwin's *Expression* book, an edition for which I was the editor. It was published in 1998, thirty-eight years after Gregory's death.

I think we can resolve our disagreement, because we are both right, each emphasizing different sides of the same coin. Emotions are not like thoughts, which need no external sign; most emotions have expressions which communicate to others. They inform us that something important is happening inside the person who shows the emotion. Those internal changes are preparing the person to deal quickly with an important event, most often some interpersonal encounter, in a way that has been adaptive in the past. The past refers to our past as individuals, and what has been adaptive in the history of our species.

We should not focus just on the signal and ignore the emotion. When we see an angry expression on someone's face, we know that person is likely to attack. The internal changes in that person's physiology are preparing them to attack;

their thinking is changing in a way that makes attacking seem to be a more useful response than if the person were not angry. (Of course the person may not attack, and perhaps that may also be detectable from his or her expression.) One of the most distinctive features of an emotion is that it is typically not hidden: we see signs of it in the expression. An emotional expression tells others something about how the person showing the expression is going to behave. That is usually useful information to the one who gets the information and the one who shows the expression.

Here the argument may get harder. Not all signals are the same; emotional expressions are special, and we should not lose sight of that. They are special because they are involuntary, not intentional. Unlike the "A-OK" or "good luck" hand gestures, emotional expressions occur without choice. Most of those who study communication, like you, Gregory, and some ethologists, have not wanted to consider intent. I believe it is crucial. The communicative value of a signal differs if it is intended or unintended. Emotional expressions have such an impact; we trust them precisely because they are unintended. We don't make an emotional expression to send a deliberate message, although a message is received. Of course, there are occasions when we use expressions deliberately for social purposes, to show agreement or disagreement, or even to lie about how we feel. My research has shown that the signal doesn't look exactly the same in these deliberate, social uses of facial expressions. We may also try to conceal our emotions, but what I have called leakage *occurs. Our emotional expressions have been shaped and preserved by evolution because they are informative, but that does not mean that we deliberately make emotional expressions to signal information to others.*

Writing about Gregory has drawn my attention to the succession of older men who took an interest in me and played a critical, *sine qua non*, role in encouraging and enabling the career I have been able to pursue. Replacing my often-cruel father, who undermined the son he called a "bum," were my two maternal uncles who gave me a year's tuition. Then Gordon Derner and Robert Berryman in graduate school, followed by Jerome Frank, my NIMH site visitor who could have been insulted about having to travel from Baltimore to Garden City, Long Island, to interview a graduate student grant applicant, but wasn't. For years to come Dr. Frank wrote letters of recommendation for me. Then came Robert Harris at Langley Porter, who invited me to come back to Langley Porter if I could get NIMH to fund a postdoctoral fellowship; then Gregory Bateson. More are to come.

The postdoctoral fellowship at Langley Porter was marvelous! I was given a small windowless room on the research floor, where everyone I met was doing research of one kind or another. I could and did talk to each of them about the research I wanted to do on nonverbal behavior. Sanford Autumn, the statistician available to all the researchers, took a special interest in my budding research program. Sanford guided me to be extra cautious. For example, when I showed people the photographs I had taken during Dr. Derner's interviews and asked them to judge whether the pictures had been taken during the stressful or cathartic portion of the interview, I showed the photographs one at a time, thirty photographs, nearly all I had taken. Did accuracy require seeing so many photographs? What would happen, Sanford probed, if I were to show each person just one photograph to judge? Would they be accurate? This was a very inefficient way to do research, getting only one data point from each person, but it was a legitimate and even interesting question, so I did the study. The people who saw only one photograph were accurate, and pooling their judgments generated the same level of accuracy I had found when each person saw thirty pictures. Over the three years of the fellowship I did fifty such experiments, closing methodological loopholes, one after another.

In the early sixties, a faculty position at UC Berkeley opened when the then well-known psychologist Nevitt Sanford moved to Stanford University. His appointment was an unusual one, involving only halftime teaching, the other halftime do research. He was paid by his faculty position to do research at the Institute of Personality and Research (IPAR), an institute that was famous in the sixties for the study of personality and creativity.

When Robert Harris recommended me for the position, IPAR invited me to come for an unusual interview. They had me sit in the center of the room, surrounded by a team of famous psychologists: Donald McKinnon, Jack Block, Frank Barron, and Richard Crutchfield. They fired questions at me, one after another. I rather liked the challenge and must have done well, for they recommended me for the appointment.

However, there was a problem. Every faculty member in psychology had to teach two courses per semester and spend at least halftime doing research, hopefully getting a grant to support that research. The position I was being recruited to fill only required teaching one course per semester, the rest of the time free for research at IPAR. Many faculty members thought this was unfair to them, and therefore had decided not to approve anyone for the post. Three times my name was put before the full faculty, and three times the majority voted against me. They then put their second choice before the faculty, and again a majority voted against it. At that point the chancellor of the university interceded, taking that faculty position away from the department.

I didn't realize how lucky I was that I didn't get that position! Instead I was able to do full-time research, with no obligation to prepare even one course a semester. I would have had to prepare from scratch three or four courses, for I would not have been able to teach the same course again and again. Preparing those courses would have eaten into my supposed halftime for research for at least a few years. Another problem I avoided was having to do the kind of research in which pieces can be broken off for students to use for their dissertations. I instead was free to do the kind of research that typically took five to ten years to complete, not having to worry if it provided opportunities for students. I had no students! For a decade I didn't have the job security that the faculty position at Berkeley would have given me, but I was free to just do research, raising my own funds to support it.

To supplement my meager postdoctoral fellowship salary I got a part-time job, teaching one course each semester to undergraduates at San Francisco State College. Lou Levine, a senior professor, had convinced the administration at SF State that every student should take a course on mental health, and that no such course offering should have more than forty students. It generated a large number of first-year psychology classes, a gold mine for me as a source of research subjects. Very few professors at SF State were doing any research at that time, and students were eager to participate in an experiment. Lou was the next in line to take an interest in me, offering me wise advice and introducing me to a fascinating woman, the comedian Mort Sahl's ex-wife, whom I suspect was more than Lou's platonic friend, but I didn't feel entitled to ask.

I found teaching very satisfying. I would teach an introduction to mental health one semester and an introduction to statistics another semester. Psychology majors had to take one course in statistics, which was frightening to most of them, and many failed that course. I became their hero when I guaranteed that any student who did all the weekly homework assignments would receive a passing grade, regardless of their score on the final test. Needless to say, those who did do all the homework passed the final test with high marks.

Teaching generated some of the same good feelings I experienced when doing psychotherapy. But I knew it was not the path I must take if I wanted to contribute to changing the world for the better, an obligation stemming from my failure to save my mother. When I later underwent psychoanalytic therapy, I realized that her suicide freed me to become independent, free of her over-controlling style. I was guilty and relieved—guilty not only for having been unable to save her, but also for benefiting from her death. My failure to save her was at the same time liberating.

CHAPTER 4

Peace Research Detour, 1961–1966

THE ARMY HAD PREPARED me for atomic warfare, which it expected to fight with field atomic weapons. I learned how to do battlefield emergency surgery on some poor goats. I was trained on how to sort casualties in atomic warfare. I also had to repeatedly practice over my two years in the army how to set up an emergency field hospital, which would be my responsibility once the war started. I advisedly did not say "if" but "when," for I was convinced we were on that path.

When I was discharged I felt an obligation to spend two years working for peace, not war. I volunteered for the American Friends Service Committee and soon became their publicist for the first nationally coordinated (eight cities simultaneously) 1961 Easter Witness for Peace. The Cold War was getting hot, with the Berlin crisis in which American and Soviet tanks faced each other separated by only a short distance, followed by the terrifying threat of the Cuban Missile Crisis.

I also organized and led the committee for Application of Behavioral Sciences to the Strategies of Peace, with the cumbersome acronym ABSSOP. The phrase "strategies of peace" was a quote from one of President Kennedy's speeches, meant to offset the implication that we might be a bunch of left-wing academics.

I enlisted nearly two hundred behavioral scientists from Bay Area universities to volunteer four hours a month to work on peace research, which I with a few colleagues was to design. In just a few years we examined the differences between those who built fallout shelters and those who formed peace groups in an article entitled "Divergent Reactions to the Threat of War,"[13] and the attitudes of state political leaders in "Coping with Cuba"[14] and "Public Opinion and the War in Vietnam."[15] For the Vietnam pieces I raised the money to hire the University of Chicago's Survey Research Center to obtain a national sample's opinions about the war, recruited the research team, contributed to the design of the questions, and did the publicity. Because we found more support for Bobby Kennedy's position on Vietnam than LBJ's we made the front page of most newspapers. I was contacted by Kennedy's people and invited to contribute towards a speech, which I did and he used.

I also articulated a policy of *balancing the bias* whenever studying an issue that had strong but differing political advocates among the scientists who might do research on the topic. I would recruit onto the research team scientists who disagreed about the policy under study. They had to agree about the design of the study and the report of the results. By preventing bias by balancing it, our intended audience of policymakers and journalists regarded our reports as reliable. In recent years I have failed to persuade those doing research on contemplative practices that they need to balance the bias of their research team by including skeptics about the benefits of meditation, as I have myself done in my few studies in this area.

Most of the research on political conflict at that time used nonzero sum bargaining games, which I suspected were too arid, devoid of emotional involvement to yield results relevant to decisions about war and peace. I designed a game heavy on emotional involvement. Professor Robert North in the political science department at Stanford had been studying how emotional factors influenced the decision to start World War I. He encouraged me apply to the Advanced Research Project Agency (ARPA) of the Department of Defense (DoD) to develop a bargaining game that built in more emotional involvement. (I was ahead of my time—in a few years, computer-based games could easily achieve that.) North (the next in the succession of good father figures) offered me half of a tenured position if either Psychology or Communications would put up the other half. Neither would, as I was, in their judgment, wasting my time studying nonverbal behavior. But my initial support from ARPA for the research on conflict was to lead, by accident, to my developing the research program for which I am best known—the cross-cultural study of facial expressions and gestures.

William Swanberg, a retired fund-raiser for the University of Chicago, heard about ABSSOP and taught me how to raise money from individual donors. (Add him and Professor North to the list of much older, wiser men who took me under their wing.) He also offered me the financial support to run for Congress for the seat to which Leo Ryan was subsequently elected. Ryan was later assassinated by Jim Jones on the airport landing strip in Guiana.

Harris Wofford, who was working for the JFK administration, invited me to meet him in Philadelphia. I must have passed his once-over, for he offered me a job as a civil rights troubleshooter in the southern United States. Another job he offered was to be the peacenik social scientist in the newly forming U.S. Government Institute of Peace.

These were very attractive choices, each offering a different way to do good in the world a lot more quickly than my beginning research on nonverbal behavior. But I had just started this research, had my first research grant, and had not much to show for it. I wanted to make at least some progress before walking away and thought mistakenly that I could return after a decade to one of these more direct political engagements. But by then those doors were closed.

After three years, with the strain of splitting my time between two universities thirty-five miles apart on unrelated subjects, and pressure from NIMH to put all my marbles in the nonverbal behavior basket if I were to obtain more support from them, I canceled my peace research detour.

CHAPTER 5

First Grant from NIMH, 1963–1966

NEAR THE END of my second fellowship year I wrote a grant proposal asking for three years to study how the nonverbal behavior of psychiatric patients changed from admission to time of discharge. Would facial expression and gesture reflect severity of illness at time of admission, would it predict who would recover, and how would it differ at time of discharge? Great questions and a grant would give me the money to not only support myself, but also hire a part-time secretary and a full-time research assistant. Most importantly, it would allow me to purchase a 16mm motion picture camera with sound, so I could really look at behavior as it unfolded. I didn't realize at the time I would also be documenting that some mentally disturbed patients, unlike my mother, could and did get well. I am amazed now that I didn't make the connection then.

When I had finished writing the grant proposal, the chairman of the psychiatry department at UCSF, Dr. Alexander Simon, would not let me submit it to the NIMH.

I was an unknown and therefore likely to be rejected, he said. And a rejection was bad for their reputation. If I put the vice-chairman's name—Dr. Leon Epstein, who was well known—as the lead investigator it would likely be funded. I would then be hired to work on *his* grant. That got my back up. I talked to the chairman of psychology at SF State where I had been teaching part-time, and asked to submit my grant through them. If it was not awarded, they would have no obligation to me; if it was funded, they would get some prestige, and I would get to run my own show and continue to teach just one course. They made the deal, and the grant was funded. Two years later, when the amounts of grant funds administered by Langley Porter dipped below the level that entitled them to receive supplemental uncommitted research funds, Simon asked me to move my research back to Langley Porter. I bargained—not only would I have to be the only named investigator, but also, if a subsequent grant was not funded, Langley Porter would have to pick up a year's salary so I could try again. A bitter pill, but he swallowed.

This time it was appropriate to send what was called a "site visitor" to examine me. The NIMH sent Lloyd Humphries, then chairman of psychology at the University of Illinois, quite a well-known experimental psychologist. He said to me that he knew nothing about nonverbal behavior, but he understood research, "so show me what you have been doing for the postdoctoral fellowship years." It was a joy! I walked him through the nearly fifty experiments I had conducted.

I got the grant and hired Patsy Garlan as my half-time secretary, who supplemented her beginning career by writing textbooks. Patsy, who later became a good friend, taught me how to write. I would write a draft, she would red pencil it, but make no changes. I would write a revision, which she would red pencil, and on and on. Now writing is what I most enjoy, a goal I never thought attainable, or even desirable, in those painful early years.

Although I have focused on the *back story* (why I chose to study a topic, how I was able to get it funded, and so forth), not the *front story* of what I found, I will make an exception to tell the front story of the **Emotional Status Exam,** since I forgot to publish it and I would like clinicians to know about it.

THE EMOTIONAL STATUS EXAM

My very first grant funded research examining the changes in nonverbal behavior that occur over the course of hospitalization in patients with severe depression. My main focus was on their responses during a standardized twelve-minute interview, which I recorded with a 16mm motion picture film camera with sound. (Twelve minutes is what a four hundred–foot magazine of film would record, more than enough to get responses to a dozen questions, such as "how are you feeling today?," "what brought you to the hospital?," and so forth.) I filmed such an interview within twenty-four hours of admission to the hospital, when the hospital staff first noticed improvement, and a week before the patient was notified that there had been sufficient improvement to merit discharge.

While the nonverbal behavior shown in those films was my main focus, before each interview began I photographed each patient in what I was to later call (at the suggestion of my colleague and close friend, the late psychiatrist Robert Rynearson) the Emotional Status Exam. I asked each patient, at the time of admission, mid-hospitalization, and discharge interviews to first sit in a chair facing a still camera. The camera lens shot through a hole cut into a mirror so the patient could see her or his face. I gave the patients a remote control and asked them to take a photograph when they thought their face was accurately showing how they were feeling. The photographs they chose to take showed despairing expressions at admission and quite contented or happy expressions at discharge. When I showed those photographs to untrained people and asked them which were taken at admission and which at discharge from a mental hospital, they achieved 100% accuracy. I should have published that, but I thought it was so obvious I forgot to do so. And yet it was evidence that facial expression conveyed accurate information, a challenge to the dogma of the time that facial expressions only displayed stereotypes.

Next I asked each patient to repeat after me each of the following sentences: "I feel sad," "I feel afraid," "I feel angry," "I feel disgusted," and "I feel happy." Each time a sentence was repeated, I asked the patient to say it again with more feeling, and then a third time with even more feeling. Most patients at time of admission broke down and cried during the sadness or fear sentence repetitions. On the anger, disgust, and happy statements they typically said, "But I don't feel that way, doctor!" The sad and fear repetitions were less intense at mid-hospitalization and even less intense at time of discharge, while the happy repetitions become stronger and more convincing over time.

Dr. Rynearson believed this simple procedure could give the clinician a quick picture of the patient's emotional status, generating recordings (now they would be less expensive videos) that could be shown and discussed with the patient. I hope someone who reads about this will do so.

It became clear that I needed more help than a single research assistant. A supplemental research grant enabled me to hire Wally Friesen to join me as the project manager, beginning what was to be twenty-five years of very fruitful collaboration and friendship.

George Mahl, a pioneer in the study of vocal signs of emotion, was trained as a research psychologist and a psychoanalyst. I visited him when he spent a year at what was then called the Stanford Center for the Study of the Behavioral Sciences, or the "Think Tank." Mahl was very kind and interested in the films of psychiatric patients I showed him. He encouraged me to focus on their "acts" and develop a theoretical classification of hand acts. It would be quite a step forward for a Skinnerian who had been schooled in not imposing theory, in simply just counting what you saw. But building on Efron's work, I developed a classification of what I called *illustrators*—five different ways that hand movements could illustrate speech as it was spoken, which Efron had described, to which I added three more. A second type of hand movement was Efron's category of what he called *emblems*, culture-specific movements that have a precise meaning known to all members of a cultural group. A third type of movement involved a hand manipulating another part of the body or the other hand, *manipulators* (which at first I called "self-adaptors," later abandoning that label because it combined description with interpretation). In the first three years, supported by my initial grant, I showed that the rate of illustrators at the time of admission to the mental hospital differentiated what were then defined as neurotic versus psychotic depressions, and the increase in illustrators at the time of discharge correlated with the psychiatrists' ratings of clinical improvement.

When I tried to get continued support for my research, as the initial grant was for only three years, my research career nearly came to an abrupt halt. I was saved by a series of lucky coincidences. The near disaster began when NIMH sent two site visitors to evaluate me and my proposal for another three years of support: Professor of Psychology Seymour Wapner and Professor of Psychiatry Herb Weiner, both very well known at the time. I had submitted as part of the proposal for renewal a lengthy progress report that included detailed descriptions about how I had begun to use motion picture film and what it had revealed that I had previously been unable to see in still photographic records. Within twenty minutes of being questioned by Wapner and Weiner, it became apparent that neither of these site visitors had read my progress report. I felt lost. They were unfriendly and impatient, asking questions that reflected their lack of preparation. I suspect I became irritated, or at least began to sulk. It was a disaster. I knew my goose was cooked!

Now I can understand a bit better why they didn't read the progress report. It was one hundred pages! I take some credit for NIMH soon thereafter placing a twelve-page limit on the length of any progress report. Too late for me. Such a page limit would have helped me focus, and maybe my site visitors would have read it. I am not certain they would have viewed my proposal more positively, since they represented the establishment that thought nonverbal behavior was a waste of time.

I had no other source of support. If the grant was not renewed, I would have had to begin the private practice of psychotherapy, literally to pay the rent and buy the food for the table. I had no savings to draw upon, no back-up job. There would be no second chance. And then, once again, luck intervened. Through nothing I planned, I was rescued. Here is how that happened.

Shortly before I wrote the application for renewing the grant, I wrote a revision of an earlier theory I had published that I thought oversimplified the type of information available from the face and body. After the new, more complex account was turned down by the prestigious journal that had gladly published the oversimplified version, I sent it to *Perceptual and Motor Skills*, a less prestigious journal. The editor, Carol Ammons, accepted it but wrote to both Silvan Tomkins and me that we had both sent articles on different aspects of nonverbal behavior, and should get to know each other. That is how Silvan and I met! I was so grateful for Ammons's gracious act that over subsequent years I never turned down her requests to review an article for her journal.

Tomkins was well known in psychology for his books on the TAT and an early book on the role of computers in psychological theory and research, but not for his magnum opus, two volumes of dense theory about affect, imagery, and consciousness. We exchanged the articles we had each submitted, and he offered to meet with me when I was next on the East Coast where he resided. I made a special trip to see him, and instead of meeting at Princeton, where he was on the faculty, he suggested we meet at ETS (Educational Testing Service), where his close friend Sam Messick, a research scholar at ETS, had given Silvan some office space. I would be given the bonus of also meeting Messick, well known at the time as a brilliant personality researcher.

I brought a 16mm film with me and showed it to both of them, explaining what I saw in the film and had begun to measure. I didn't know, nor do I think did Silvan, that Sam was a member of the group that would a few months later review my application to renew my grant. I was to learn, much later, that when Sam heard the negative report from Wapner and Weiner, with a recommendation to reject my application, he objected. He said he had seen one of my films and was impressed with my promise. To resolve this disagreement the review committee agreed to abide by the judgment of an outside consultant, and who did they pick?—George Mahl, the person I would have asked them to pick if I had been in on it. The grant was renewed. Never again did I ever let my fate depend on just one grant; I always made certain to have two or sometimes three grants going.

What a string of coincidences saved my bacon. If not for Ammons, I would not have met Tomkins. If not for Tomkins, I would not have met Messick. If not for Messick, the committee would have rejected my proposal. And if not for Mahl's having earlier that year seen my films, he might not have been so enthusiastic when asked to resolve the disagreement about whether my research career should be continued.

So much good luck! For so long I wanted to believe it was up to me, not luck. But, without the luck I would have failed, and this coincidence of luck, talent, and perseverance repeats again and again throughout my life. As an adolescent my favorite poem was a verse from Henley's poem "Invictus":

It matters not how straight the gate,/

How charged with punishment the scroll,/

I am the master of my fate:/

I am the captain of my soul./

It is only in the last two decades of my life that I came to see how much this captain depended on good fortune, lucky breaks!

Here is another one. I was supporting myself by paying my salary from one or another grant. I heard that NIMH had a program called the Career Scientist Awards, which was designed to support young scientists developing their career, and a follow-up program designed to rescue active scientists from teaching and administration to instead be able to continue to pursue research. They offered five years of salary support, but a long application was required and less than forty were funded at any one time; many less each application period.

The application required you to plan what you would be doing for the next five years. I was funded on my initial application for a Career Scientist Award, and then again six more times, for a total of thirty-five years. Having that support freed me from the vagaries of being dependent on individual research grants for my salary. It gave me precious security until 1972 when I was given a tenured faculty position at UCSF (the unusual way that came about I will explain later). I continued to have Career Scientist Awards during my professorship, until two years before I retired in 2004. Instead of adding it to my salary, I gave the career awards' yearly funding to my department to recompense them for my not serving on any committees or doing any teaching (the terms of the award required such a commitment to only do research), which is exactly what I wanted! The Career Scientist Award program continues, but it is no longer possible to have an award renewed for more than ten years.

Two people ran the program when I first applied, Bert Boothe and Betty Pickett. After my second application was funded, I looked up Betty during one of my many visits to NIMH, in order to express my thanks. On the wall behind her was a painting by Robert Natkin. Natkin and I were friends when we were both students in Chicago, he at the Art Institute and me at the University. When he moved to New York City in the 1950s, renting a large loft, I wired it for him, as it only had ceiling lights. He gave me a large painting to express his thanks. Natkin became a renowned painter, and when I sold it to the local museum, the painting he gave me allowed me to purchase a country house.

I told Betty that I knew Natkin and owned two of his paintings (one was the gift) and a watercolor. The watercolor was also a gift and the second painting I bought at a large discount. We probably would have become friends without the Natkin connection, but the friendship thrived.

Betty was twelve years older than me, and over time she encouraged and advised me many times.

After I had been on a career award for twenty years, the program had a stake in me. I was one of their most successful investments, and they wanted me to thrive, discover, and publish, which I did. Add Betty and Margaret Tresselt (who gave me my first taste of research when I was an undergraduate) to the list of older mentors who took me under their wing.

In 1966, Silvan had moved to the City University of New York Graduate Center, opposite the public library at Fifth Avenue and Forty-Second Street. He bargained for and received three thousand square feet of very expensive space at this location for a research laboratory. The only problem was that Silvan did not know how to do laboratory research. To solve this problem, he convinced City University to offer me a tenured associate professorship to create and run a laboratory on facial expression. They paid for me to spend a full month in New York, getting to know the setting, before I had to make a decision.

I had already submitted my first application for a career award to NIMH, but had not yet learned the outcome of the review. But, at best it was for five years, and City University was offering me lifetime support. I wouldn't be in San Francisco, but I would have the opportunity to be able to talk to Silvan about the work I would do.

When I returned to San Francisco, I wrote NIMH telling them I was withdrawing my application for the career award to take the position at City University. Bert Boothe, who was head of the fellowships branch of NIMH, under which the Career Award program fell, called Enoch Calloway, the director of research at Langley Porter, telling him to tell me that for reasons he could not disclose, based on information he had about City University, it would be a terrible mistake for me to accept the position at City University. He would not withdraw my application for the career award, and I should know that I would shortly be officially told it was approved.

It was like hearing a message from Mount Olympus. NIMH had spoken, had warned me, and had told me what to do. Although I had already sent a letter of acceptance to City University a few weeks earlier, I notified them I had changed my mind. As it turned out, within a year from when I would have arrived, City University was in chaos, disrupted by divisive arguments about the merits of adopting a new policy of open admissions. I narrowly avoided being swallowed up in that chaos. Add Bert Boothe to the list of older people who looked after me.

CHAPTER 6

Cross-Cultural Research, 1966–1971

IT WASN'T MY IDEA to do this research. I was asked—pushed. I didn't even write the research proposal. It was written for me by the man who gave me the money to do it.

After a year of research on threats (in the political science department at Stanford) I went back to D.C. to meet with the then head of behavioral sciences at ARPA (whom I will refer to only by his first name, Lee), a branch of the Defense Department, to ask for another year's support. Lee told me there would be no more support for game or bargaining research, and asked what else I was doing. I said he wouldn't be interested, but after strong encouragement I described my fledgling research on nonverbal behavior. Lee told me that he was married to a woman from Thailand and thought some of their marital problems were due to cross-cultural nonverbal misunderstandings. He then asked if I would like to figure out what was the same and what was different across cultures in nonverbal behavior. It had to be basic research, no military application, and I would have to do all of the out-of-the-country research myself, no subcontracting it to others. He could fund whatever it would cost! I said I would think about it and get back to him.

When I returned the next day to San Francisco, I decided not to pursue Lee's invitation. I did not know how to do cross-cultural research; I did not even know what the arguments were, the literature, or the methods. I thought it best to stick to my by then two NIMH grants. Two days later Lee called to find out how the proposal was coming, and when he learned that I had decided not to pursue it, he said he would see me the next day in San Francisco. Lee sat for a day in my office, and wrote the proposal he then funded that allowed me to do the research I am best known for—evidence for the universality of some facial expressions of emotion, and cultural differences in gestures. Lee gave me close to a million dollars. That was a lot of money in 1965 dollars; it would be seven million in 2015 dollars.

I found out many years later the true reason he had dumped so much money on me. It wasn't because of his wish to fix his marital problems, or even curiosity. He had to get rid of money quickly because Senator Frank Church had caught him using social science research as a cover for getting information in Chile that could be used to overthrow the then left-wing government of President Allende. Lee had money earmarked for overseas research, and he had to spend it quickly, before the end of the fiscal year, or he wouldn't get as much money the next year. And I walked through his door. An innocent who could do overseas research that wouldn't get him into trouble!

My first step was to visit individually the major players on this issue. Tomkins, a universalist I already knew, and Charles Osgood, a psychologist who was very famous for his research on the meaning of words, having developed the *Semantic Differential*, a tool used in many studies by many others. I knew Charlie from his peace research, and we had become more than acquaintances. But, with no interest in words I had not become an acolyte. Charlie had published a study using the semantic differential to judge what was shown in photographs of facial expression. He thought it would be great to do such a study in different cultures. I thought his approach was too far removed from understanding the nonverbal behavior itself.

On the other side of the aisle was Ray Birdwhistell, a linguist who had published a theory of *kinesics*, proposing to apply linguistic analysis to nonverbal behavior. He had convinced some psychiatrists to use his notational system to describe patient behavior. I went to visit him and asked to see his findings documenting the cultural differences in nonverbal behavior, which he had heralded in his book. It was all in his head, he said.

My next stop was Edward T. Hall, the anthropologist who coined the term *proxemics* to describe the distances people maintain between each other. While I had no doubt then or now that such differences exist, he neither had any documentation, nor anything to say about facial expression.

Margaret Mead was more difficult to reach, rejecting my initial request for a meeting. Through the intervention of her ex-husband, Gregory Bateson, she finally agreed to meet, telling me she had nothing to add to Ray

Birdwhistell. There was no controversy to be settled, she told me. The evidence was in: Birdwhistell had proven that there are no universals in expression. Mead was cold, impatient, not giving me much time, treating me like a fool.

With Silvan Tomkins's advice, using photographs from his collection that he selected to best exemplify six emotions—anger, disgust, fear, happiness, sadness, and surprise—I launched a series of studies in which I showed these photographs to people in other cultures, asking them to choose from among a list of six emotion terms the one that best fit each facial expression. I did not know then that I was using a method that Darwin had been the first to use, as I had not yet seen a reason to read Darwin's book.

If I had read Darwin's book I would have learned that when he showed photographs of expressions to people he allowed them to describe the emotion they perceived in their own words, rather than limiting their choice to six emotion terms as I did. His method is a better one than mine, for the discovery of what emotion is signaled by an expression, as no bias is introduced that might influence how people label a facial expression. Consider for a moment an experiment in which I might show a facial expression that actually is a signal of sadness, but the choices among which people had to choose were compassion, anger, fear, disgust, or surprise. They would likely choose compassion most frequently. But if I were to allow them to say in their own words what the face conveys, sad related words would appear most frequently and compassion rarely.

To this day, psychologists studying expressions fail to inquire what people say, but instead use the method I used, of limiting their choices. It makes the subsequent analysis of the responses much faster to tally. Fortunately, we do not have to rely just upon what emotion terms are chosen to label facial expressions to demonstrate universality. I also used quite different methods to tackle this problem.

I think it is important to know that when I did the initial studies in 1966–1967 showing people photographs and asking them to choose from a list which emotion each photograph conveyed, I did not know what to expect. I knew Silvan claimed universality, but he had no more evidence than Birdwhistell. It was an open question. I didn't yet care which way it came out, so long as I could help resolve the disagreement and find out who was right.

I went to Brazil and Argentina, and arranged to get judgments from students in Chile to compare with the judgments of Americans, and later with Japanese students. There were no differences across these cultures in the words they chose for each photograph.

Tomkins kept secret that he was encouraging another psychologist, Carol Izard, to do exactly the same study, using other photographs supplied by Tomkins and obtaining judgments from students in other cultures. We didn't know that we were replicating each other's work! We each thought that we, alone, were obtaining the first cross-cultural evidence on facial expression. When we discovered Tomkins's duplicity, he explained it was better for the science, to have the work repeated independently. No matter our bruised career ambitions.

I am surprised now that I accepted his explanation so easily and continued what became a very close, intimate friendship, almost like father and intellectual son, until another duplicitous act a decade later caused me to stop all contact with him a few years before his death. I will explain the rupture in our perhaps too close relationship later.

I invited Izard to join me in jointly presenting our findings at the next meeting of the American Psychological Association, which he did, to defuse any possible rivalry about who got the evidence on universality first. Nevertheless, we had from thereon a relationship plagued by rivalry. I did not share with Izard my doubts about our findings. There was a gaping loophole through which I thought any cultural relativist, like Birdwhistell, would be able to march in triumph once he found out what we had learned. Closing that loophole required finding people who had never had the opportunity to learn which facial expressions signaled which emotions by seeing outsiders or the media. For if they were to interpret facial expression the same way in which people in literate cultures did, but were not visually isolated, it might not be their evolutionary heritage but seeing John Wayne and Charlie Chaplin that was responsible for their choices. That I suspected would be Birdwhistell's or Margaret Mead's rebuttal, and so, anticipating it, I had to see if I could close that loophole by studying a visually isolated people.

I first went to the Mayan peninsula, having heard from Fred Strodbeck, a professor at the University of Chicago who ran a field research station in Merida, that there were off-the-road villages where people had not seen movies or TV. Through his generosity and advice, I began to hike into such villages, going in different directions each day. Again and again I found magazines showing facial expressions, despoiling the visual isolation, if not the occasional visits of entertainers who used batteries and generators to very occasionally show a movie. I had no luck!

Through acquaintances I had made from organizing peace protests for the Quakers, I became friends with Sadja Goldsmith (who had just begun a career in Planned Parenthood) and her then husband, Bob, who specialized in tropical medicine. When, at the dinner table, he heard tales of my repeated failures in the jungles of Maya to find visually isolated people, he told me who already had just what I needed: Carleton Gajdusek, a neurologist at the National Institutes of Health (NIH) who had film records of two visually isolated cultures in the highlands of Papua New Guinea. I wrote Gajdusek, who invited me to visit him at NIH. When he found out in detail what I was after he lent me copies of over two hundred hours of silent 16mm film that the cinematographer he had hired, E. Richard Sorenson, and he had recorded of two different cultures in New Guinea. Neither he nor Sorenson had yet had the time to look at the films, but I was welcome to do so. He guaranteed that the people I would see had seen very few outsiders, no photographs, no magazines, no films, etc.

Carleton's appearance was incongruous. He sported a youthful crew-cut (out of fashion by then), and was clothed informally, appropriate to a twenty-year-old from the 1950s rather than the director of an important and very well-funded laboratory. Carleton was restless, always on the move with agile quick movements that belied his forty-four years. His resting facial countenance was slightly quizzical, abruptly glancing at me sideways, peering for only a moment in a penetrating fashion.

In our initial meeting he seemed ill at ease. Was he nervous, ambivalent about inviting an outsider into his territory, or was this his usual manner? One never knows on a first encounter what is a stable part of that person's idiosyncratic behavior, or germane to what is happening and being felt at the moment. His actions—the loan of the film and the invitation to work in his area with the aid of his facilities—fit my ideal of what a scientist should do. But there was something about his manner that suggested that Carleton might resent anyone who he thought was using him to discover something about *his* people. True, he wasn't studying facial expression of emotion, but I hadn't spent a decade setting up the facilities that would enable my work. I did not know enough about the medical tradition for handling such situations to suggest that I would include his name on any publications. That is not the tradition in psychology, where such help is acknowledged in a footnote, not an authorship credit. None of these thoughts entered my mind then, just uneasiness.

Carleton did not tell me that there were other medical researchers (e.g., M. Alpers) and an anthropologist (S. Lindebaum) who had been and were continuing to study Kuru, a degenerative disease endemic to Papua New Guinea. Carleton received the Nobel Prize in 1976 (nine years after my work in the New Guinea) for his research on Kuru, helping establish that it was spread by cannibalism and that it incubated for some years before it became symptomatic.

Stanley Prusiner, who had an antagonistic relationship with Gajdusek, having proven Gajdusek wrong for his explanation of Kuru despite winning the Nobel Prize, received the Nobel Prize in 1997 for an alternative explanation of the causes of Kuru, which has held up to scientific scrutiny. Here is Prusiner's description of his first impressions of Carleton, whom he calls the "guru of kuru," and whom he notes the New Guineans called "Dr. America."

> *[He] . . . was an engaging, forceful, insecure individual whose rambunctious personality remained unaltered throughout the thirty-four years of our acquaintance. . . . He was addicted to hyperbole, and he loved hearing his own baritone voice; he was driven to dominate every conversation in any room he found himself. . . . A masterful speaker, he was famous for his three- or four-hour-long lectures; he could keep an audience spellbound. He also polarized people: Some of his colleagues were devoted . . . others annoyed by his wild exaggerations and rambling monologues found him difficult.*

Carleton was working in the southeast Highlands of New Guinea, because only the people in this small area of New Guinea were dying of Kuru. Nearly 40 percent of the approximately twenty thousand Fore (pronounced Foray) people were afflicted. Carleton was trying to find out the nature of the disease and the means of transmission. Was it infectious contact or cannibalism? The Fore were known to eat the corpses of people they had loved or respected. The Fore believed Kuru was the result of someone casting a spell on you.

Halfway through my first trip to New Guinea, when I was living by myself in a village, the chief started to squeeze my thigh as a crowd gathered, jumping up and down with excitement, yelling something that sounded like "whay." Later I found out that the chief had said that if I died he would eat me. The excitement was not that they were about to kill me, an interpretation I quickly discarded since they seemed so friendly. But could those smiles be at the anticipation of getting rid of this stranger? No, I was too entertaining, showing off such magic as matches or a flashlight. They were excited because the chief's announcement that he would eat me if I died meant I was now a respected man.

From a public health standpoint, cannibals are safer if they eat their enemies, not their friends. Enemies are likely to be in good shape, killed in battle, while at least some friends die of disease, which could be easily transmitted. The South Fore didn't cook the friends they ate; the brain was considered an essential part of the meal. The women and children were the most avid cannibals, and they, more than the men, were victims of Kuru.

Gajdusek also wanted the brains of Kuru victims to ship back to Bethesda for study. He rewarded them with blankets for the loss of their respected friend's brain. I never knew if they thought Gajdusek was eating the brains of their friends once he was alone. There was no treatment for Kuru then or later. Once a person began to shake with the first symptoms of the disease, it meant certain death months later. Kuru disappeared many years later when the Australian public health doctors (that part of New Guinea became an Australian trust territory after World War II) succeeded in getting the people to stop eating each other by offering them steel axes if they abstained.

Before I went to New Guinea I carefully studied the films Carleton had given me. It took more than six months. I stopped the film whenever there was a clear shot of someone's facial expression. Using my fancy, expensive slow-motion film projectors I would rewind and look again at the expression in slow motion, and then again in real time. Wally Friesen and I never saw a facial expression we had not encountered in our own lives; one point for Charles Darwin. If Margaret Mead was right we should have seen very different culturally unique expressions. There were none.

A dedicated cultural relativist could argue that Carleton had ignored any expressions that were unique to the South Fore, only filming what was familiar. Two counter arguments: often these expressions happened so quickly that there would have been no way for him to anticipate what was going to happen next; and, Carleton had a vested interest in what was unique to these people, not what was universal. Still another objection could have been that it didn't matter that they showed familiar expressions if those familiar expressions signaled entirely different information than they did in literate cultures. Ray Birdwhistell had not argued that people in other cultures didn't smile; just that their smiles were not in any way related to enjoyment. But our impressions contradicted that claim. Whenever we could see what happened before the expression or right after, it confirmed that our Western interpretation of these New Guineans expressions was correct. Two points for Darwin. There were bodily gestures we hadn't seen before such as grasping each shoulder with the opposite hand, but Darwin had said gestures were socially learned and culturally variable—point three.

Up until viewing Gajdusek's films I was not certain who was right, Darwin or Mead. I was trained during a period in psychology when the influence of biology was dismissed as irrelevant, when no one considered evolutionary thinking. The received knowledge heralded in the textbooks was that scientific psychology had proven laymen wrong in their belief that expressions provided reliable information. They were all stereotypes. Just like thinking the world was flat because that is how it appeared. (Some years later I carefully analyzed[16] the experiments that had led to that faulty conclusion, revealing many defects in each of them.) Silvan Tomkins (I described our meeting in chapter 5) had just published an article suggesting that facial expressions do provide reliable information, but that didn't prove they were universal.

Worried that our judgments of the emotions shown in the Sorenson/Gajdusek films might have been influenced by what the films showed of the preceding and subsequent behavior, we edited excerpts that showed only the expression, not the context. I brought Silvan out to San Francisco and showed him these excerpts. His judgments were the same as mine had been.

If I was an ethologist, like Eibl-Eibesfeldt, I would have stopped with what I had identified in the Sorenson/Gajdusek films. It would be evidence enough. An anthropologist might also consider it sufficient proof, but not a research psychologist. There was no control for observer bias. The cameraman had chosen what to record. There was no way to know if he had ignored frequent examples of culture-specific facial expressions.

Convinced by my study of Gajdusek's films that Tomkins, and Darwin before him, was right, I nevertheless knew that what I had seen in the films was suggestive, not definitive. I had to go to New Guinea myself and obtain systematic, quantitative evidence safeguarded from any unwitting bias if I was to challenge powerful relativists like Mead. So, in 1967 I began to plan a trip with almost no idea of what I would find and what I would do once I was there, only what was missing. I had to find a way to do experiments on facial expression with people who had never seen outsiders, who were still using stone implements, and who had no written language. What an exciting challenge!

I prepared photographic materials to bring—stills of facial expressions I pulled off of the movies of these people, in case they would not be able to make sense of Caucasian expressions from Tomkins's collection, which I also brought. But what if they couldn't make sense of photographs, as some anthropologists had claimed about other visually isolated peoples? I knew I didn't know what I would do. I would find out. I was about to go off on an adventure into the unknown, living my boyhood dream of walking in Magellan's footsteps of exploration.

Of course there were no direct flights. The trip from San Francisco to the Highlands village of Goroka took four days. I took a break for a few days in Goroka, surrounded by nearly naked Highland peoples. Finally, I made the arrangements to meet Carleton Gajdusek at a missionary's tiny landing area in the South Fore area. The only way to get there was to charter a single-engine, two-person airplane. I didn't want to do it. I already felt unsafe in commercial airlines, struggling with my anxiety about being above the ground, but a flight on a tiny airplane was even scarier. And, it turned out my fear was justified.

Just after we reached our cruising altitude of a few thousand feet, the pilot told me that the conning tower at this tiny airport in Goroka just radioed that one of our wheels had dropped off after take-off. We had to return to the airport where they had fire-dousing equipment.

There was no sign of fear on the face of this eighteen-year-old bush pilot when he said our single-engine Cessna may catch fire as we dug and slid our way into the ground, just to the side of the paved runway. He told me to practice opening and closing the door by my side now, even though we were thousands of feet up in the air, so I would be able to snap it open a moment before we hit. This was to prevent the door from jamming on impact and imprisoning me in the cockpit that might catch fire. I did so, holding the door open for a few moments, unable to resist the impulse to look down, and then closing it.

All my life until now I had gone out of my way to avoid what I then did. When I opened that door and looked down, I could easily have leaped to my death if I had been seized by an overwhelming impulse to jump. When I was a child that is exactly what my mother said I would do when I grew up because I was so evil. As protection from her prophecy, I had not before put myself in a position where I might act out her prediction so quickly.

We circled the landing field once, prepared to land on the next turn. My fingers clenched the door handle, but I felt no fear. In fact I felt very calm. As a student of emotion I wondered why I was not afraid. I should have been since I was anticipating death or injury. It must have been because I had something to do. Too bad I couldn't run an experiment in which I would be just a witness, with someone else holding the door. With no way to cope with the danger, nothing to do, I bet I would have been terrified.

Maybe I was not afraid because I had no obligations to anyone, in that sense nothing to lose. At thirty-three I was divorced, no children, no lover, a dead mother, a father that I blamed for her death, estranged from my sister. I had no connections other than to my work. The study I was about to do in New Guinea turned out to be one of the most important and most controversial in my career. I knew it could be. While the risk of finding nothing conclusive was great, if my evidence was strong, it could settle a century-old dispute about facial expressions. I thought this was a once-in-a lifetime opportunity—it was and I was eager to seize it.

When we slid into the grass on the side of the runway, I hopped out. The plane was damaged, but no fire. We unloaded my gear, put it into another Cessna, and took off again. While we cruised not high above the ground I looked out at the dense foliage, occasionally interrupted by small clusters of grass-roofed huts and small terraced gardens. My excitement mounted steadily. Thirty minutes later we landed. After tea with the missionary, Carleton and I set off.

We drove off on a very bumpy semblance of a road to Okapa in Carleton's Land Rover, too noisy and bumpy to talk. There I meet the local Australian public health doctors John Matthews and Neville Hoffman.

From my diary kept at the time:

> . . . *Carleton spent the next five hours telling tales of terror and gossip. I learned that the Cessnas are extremely hazardous, that two weeks ago one crashed taking off at*

Goroka, that a month ago one crashed landing at Tarabu, that in fact there were six fatal accidents in the last few months. Also that I might get on Carleton's list of Europeans exposed to Kuru who he hoped (jokingly?) would be the first Caucasians to get the disease.

I was more than uneasy at the undercurrent of his conversation. While I began to think I could not trust Carleton, I didn't want to believe that, for how was I going to get along without him? I also sensed that there was something peculiar in his intimacy with the New Guinea boys who always surrounded him. [I was not surprised when thirty years later I read in the New York Times *that Carleton had been convicted of sexually molesting one of the boys he had brought back to America to live with him. In his New Guinea journals, published by NIH, Carleton had written about the virtues of man-boy sex. He sent copies of these very thick journals chronicling his travels, findings, and beliefs to various scientists and anyone else who asked for them, but no one, including me, read them, until a pedophile must have come across them, for he posted on a website, monitored by the FBI, the hot stuff in one of Carleton's journals, easily ordered from NIH.]*

Carleton was arrested in 1996 for child molestation. In 1997 a plea bargain specified that he spend nine to twelve months in jail, five years afterwards abroad. He is the only Nobel Prize winner (shared for his discoveries on degenerative brain diseases) to be convicted of a felony, spending time in jail at the age of seventy-four. There were only hints then. I still had not reached the stage in my own development when I would trust rather than pooh-pooh my hunches.

I spent the next few days around the hospital in Okapa, trying to get the natives who had come there to see a relative or for treatment to look at my pictures of facial expressions. A boy who had been to a missionary school [and] who had learned Pidgin would translate my rudimentary knowledge of Pidgin into the South Fore language. As a native looked at a photograph, he would ask him if it showed the person was "kros" (angry), "laikam" (happy), "poreit" (afraid), or sad (I have lost my record of the word used). There is no Pidgin for surprise, disgust, or contempt, so instead they were told "he sees something new," "he looks at something bad or stinks," I didn't try to offer anything for contempt.

Most of the people we tested didn't seem to understand what we were asking them to do. Maybe the problem was that they had to keep in mind a number of words to reach their decision. In our previous research in literate cultures, people read a list of words, from which they could choose one for each picture they viewed. They didn't have to rely on memory when they were evaluating the emotion shown in a facial expression. In a preliterate culture we couldn't do that. A few natives were able to handle the task, giving responses similar to those I had found in literate cultures, but it wouldn't matter, for they had extensive contact with Westerners.

Again from my diary, fifth day in New Guinea:

I am beginning to wonder what I am doing here. I certainly won't understand the culture in my limited time. My filming of them won't be worth much, at best just more anecdotes, and the responses to the pictures I show them are ones of confusion. Once here there is an almost irresistible urge to seek after the primitive, the true, the uncontaminated native. Yesterday and even more today I find thoughts of unhappy love affairs intruding into my consciousness. Last night while sleeping on the floor I dreamed I was marrying Elaine May [I knew her only by sight when we were both at the University of Chicago decades earlier]. I am feeling quite disappointed about all the time and money, what it will yield.

I started to ask, through my schoolboy Pidgin translators, some of the natives to show me the emotions on their own face. It is almost impossible to get one person alone, and others distract and embarrass the person I am filming. I am beginning to feel crawly-buggy, probably fleas.

This adventure is curing me of being a breast-man. I saw more breasts today than I have seen previously in my life—about twenty times as many. Already they have lost their allure. What a price to pay for science!

A few days later I got my chance to see people who were truly visually isolated. Carleton and I hiked into a village where a man was dying of Kuru to wait for his death so Carleton could get his brain for study back at NIH. The hike was long; I was not accustomed to the altitude, about 7500 feet. I stumbled along, rather quickly losing sight of Gajdusek and the train of cargo carriers. The path was sometimes slippery with soft mud often covering my boots with each step. I had been told that there were snakes with deadly venom, another hazard to fear. The plants of spear-like grass, sharp on the edges were higher than my head. When I slipped, I sometimes grabbed the grass to keep from going head first into the mud, rewarded by fine, paper-like cuts on my hands.

At one point I came to a chasm, with only a log providing the means across. The drop appeared to be more than one hundred feet. I was paralyzed. I am afraid of heights, but I didn't think I could find my way back. I inched my way across on my belly, clinging to the log and cursing myself and Carleton.

From my diary:

I entered the village about two hours after Carleton and the "boys." In Pidgin, white people are called "mastas" and natives are called "boys," reflecting the colonial origin of Pidgin. We are living in a thatched hut in the center of this small hamlet. The hut was built for us yesterday. Right now there are about fifteen boys and men watching us while I type and Carleton is reading Moby Dick. *Everyone gets excited when the bell rings when the typewriter carriage comes to the end. I am making music, rather monotonous, but novel for them. So far I have gotten two natives to look at my photographs of expressions. I don't know whether my explanation in my very rough Pidgin of the task was comprehensible to them. I am discouraged, although less right now than I was earlier today. The experience is exotic, but I don't think I am going to learn much. When I think of the time invested in preparing to come here and now, I feel very sad about what I am getting out of it: almost nothing. I am plagued and worried by the question of how can I retrieve more from this venture, but I have come up with nothing so far.*

There is little danger. The people are friendly and the living (even here in the hamlet) is not too bad. The food is dreadful, like eating the part of the asparagus we discard. The sleeping is a bit hard, but not much worse than camping in the Sierras. I worry occasionally about getting Kuru, but malaria is probably more likely. The disappointment is that I had some magical expectation that once here I would know just what to do and learn all sorts of wonderful things. If it was not for the embarrassment of admitting I have made a mistake and the problem of explaining to everyone, I would leave.

I am struck by the terrible contrast between the lives of the people in this village and ours. Since we've arrived we have been listening to music, drinking wine, and playing cards. What must they think of these "mastas" who pay them in order to cut up a member of their family who dies of sorcery? Yet the relatives of a patient dying in a hospital in the States (if the visitors' room was adjacent to the interns' rest area) would have a similar shock.

In the middle of the night I was awakened by something wet falling on my face and a loud noise. Carleton had moved the autopsy table from the center of the room, close to where I was sleeping. The noise that awakened me was Carleton sawing off the skull to get the brain out of the Kuru victim who had died in the middle of the night. The wet matter hitting my face was bits of bone and brain. I screamed, "Carleton, what are you doing?" "Congratulations," he replied, "you have now had infectious contact with Kuru!" I was furious, but said nothing, crawling away from him, determined I would no longer put myself in jeopardy. I didn't know how I would do it, but I would have to work on my own.

I didn't fall back to sleep, worried that I might get Kuru if a bit of brain had entered my open mouth while I slept. [In

1976 when my ten years of possible incubation were up I was quite relieved I had missed getting Kuru.]

When we got back to the hospital in Okapa, I worked some more with schoolboys who translated from Pidgin into Fore. Often the people we examined had considerable contact with the outside, but occasionally someone who hadn't would come by. Sometimes they chose an emotion word that made sense, sometimes not. How they responded was not related to how much contact they had had. Was it the translator, how smart they were, or how well they could adapt to the strange situation, never encountered before, of seeing photographs of expressions and saying something about that person? I had no way to know.

After a week, Dick Sorenson, Gajdusek's cinematographer, suggested that I move to a thatched "house" in Wanitabe, where he could provide me with a couple of schoolboy Pidgin translators. Living there for a few weeks was fascinating. The people were friendly, and I was an enormously interesting curiosity, from my clothing to my gadgets. They didn't understand what a camera did, soon getting accustomed to my walking around the center of the village with this odd object held up to my face most of the time. Even the nubile women, unclothed from the waist up, grew accustomed to my presence. Both men and women wore only short grass skirts or weavings. Pleasant during the days, at seven thousand feet it was cold at night, so they huddled in their huts around a fire. With no chimney they were covered with soot, which they didn't wash off very often as there was no nearby source of water. Water was brought in from more than a mile away in bamboo tubes.

A few times a week there was what seemed to be a common picnic in the center of the village in which they cooked taro, pit-pit another stalk, and other vegetables they grew in the gardens. The women did the farming—they were the tractors—while the men maintained the fences surrounding the villages to keep the pigs in, not out. Pigs were pets, valued also as the equivalent of money, and occasionally slaughtered, for a "sing-sing," in which an entire village would celebrate something. The pig was not very well cooked, but because the opportunity to eat it was so rare, it was highly valued. I had to use subterfuge to accept but not eat the pig meat offered to me at a sing-sing.

I filmed and photographed boys playing, throwing grass spears at each other in mock battle. I often got films of people meeting those they knew, accompanied by broad smiles, arms stretched out, and hands grasping each other's shoulders. Man to man, woman to woman, never man to woman. Sorenson told me that adultery was common; occurring in the bush, literally, since there was no other place to find privacy. Killings occurred when someone was discovered in the act. This was substantiated by the village elder's account, translated for me, of someone who had attacked a man whom he discovered with his woman. He tried to get that man to re-enact it for me, with no luck. One day I walked to a neighboring village, filming the terror on a child's face when she first saw an outsider. I got a nice picture of disgust on the face of an old man witnessing me eating a can of food I had gotten from a missionary. One of the days Sorenson visited, we asked the elder to give us a concert on one of their instruments that resembled a Jew's harp. Children gathered for the treat of listening to the music. My motion picture camera was running when we played back from an audiotape recorder the music he had just made. They had never before heard anything coming out of a recorder, not knowing that could be done. I got a wonderful example of surprise, followed by excitement and enjoyment.

Most of the days I was alone in the sense there was no one to talk to except for the schoolboys, with whom I couldn't hold a conversation beyond a few words in Pidgin. Alone in terms of conversation, I was never physically alone. When I went to sleep at night, a dozen men and boys sat watching me, who were replaced by others sitting and watching me when I awoke in the morning. The only time I was alone was when I went to the "little-house," a shack built over the edge of a crevice. A rope hung down, which you grasped while leaning out to defecate into the pit. A slip and you were literally buried in shit. I was careful.

I had never before been alone for so long, with no one to talk to for weeks. I considered what I was doing with my life. Work was fine, although I was frustrated by not figuring out how to study emotion in these people, but a personal life didn't exist. I determined that I would seek to marry again and this time have children. After ten years since my first marriage, seven since our divorce, followed by two failed relationships and a host of casual affairs, I felt it was time to be ready to make a commitment.

I listened again and again to the Beatles' *Sgt. Pepper's Lonely Hearts Club Band*, which I had transferred to tape before traveling. I felt like the "Fool on the Hill," which I played over and over. I had launched a study of the symbolic gestures in use by these people, which was going well, but not the work on facial expressions. Asking them to choose an emotion word for each picture seemed very frustrating to most people. I tried a matching task, in which I laid out a photograph of each of the six emotions, held up a photograph of another expression, asking them, through my Pidgin translators, to match the emotion shown in the new one with one of the six laid out in front of them. This seemed to work no better. I then tried asking them to make up a story about each photograph, telling me what had happened before to cause this expression, and what the person was going to do next.

From my diary:

It seemed very difficult to get across the idea that they should describe an emotion. Instead they used the picture as a starting point for telling a story. . . . Despite this problem, on almost half of the stimuli they gave the predicted response. Where they deviated their story usually represents a minor error in perception [e.g., a fear story to a surprise photograph, or vice versa]. The problem in working with bushy people is to get across affect perception. If we could, the best idea would be to make up some stories which are related to each affect for the Fore and then have them choose between stories when looking at a photograph. [That is pretty close to the task that I used the following year, but I hadn't thought of it yet.]

There are three almost inseparable problems which contaminate the results. First, whether the subject understands the task, whether he grasps the concept of describing feelings. On the matching task the failure to get the task concept is most important when they match on the basis of open-close mouth rather than affect. The second problem is the willingness to report what they see or think; inhibitions to reveal information about embarrassing or taboo topics. The third problem is, of course, the opportunity to have learned the stimuli for the affect by watching Europeans. The less likely problem is three, by getting informants in the bush, the more likely problems are one and two. [Elsewhere in my diary I noted a fourth problem: that the translators were either incompetent or uninterested in reporting accurately.]

The results with the story-telling task, which was the most difficult task but yielded the best results with the bushy subjects, and the task in which they had to choose a word for each expression, were more consistent with the universals than the culture-specific viewpoint. While the findings were statistically significant they weren't as strong as I had hoped to obtain. Convinced I would make no further progress, I left after a month, hoping to return once I had figured out a task that would be easier to comprehend and required no translator.

The day after I left I wrote:

Generally it's been a worthwhile trip. From a work point of view it was quite worthwhile. Personally, it had its ups and downs; there were some extremely depressing days, and some severe physical hardships, but I also made some very good friends [I was referring here to Neville Hoffman, one of the Australian public health doctors]. And the Fore people are extraordinary and friendly and enchanting. Carleton is impossible. He has been away from NG for the last 20 days which is why I was able to get something done!

A few months after my return it hit me. I could read them a few lines describing an emotion-inducing event, lay out three pictures, and ask them to point to the one that fit the story. They would not have to say a word, just point. There would be no worry about having exact correct translations of single emotions words, such as anger or fear, as long as I had good translations of the stories. I checked the literature on studies of children before they could read, finding "my" task had been first used by a long-forgotten psychologist, Dashiel, in 1927. I wasn't disappointed that I had not been the first to think of this. It confirmed my belief that it would work with people who had no written language.

The stories I would be reading to them in this new task were culled from the answers they had given when I asked them to give me a story for each of the expressions. I used the most common ones, stripping them down to the bare essentials: seeing friends (for happiness); seeing something new (surprise); about to fight (angry); child has died (sadness); and seeing something that smells bad (disgust). Fear presented more of a problem for their stories had elements of surprise or anger. I constructed the following story: you are in your hut and a wild pig is standing at the entrance. He has been standing there for a long time (no surprise). You are thinking he is going to attack, but you have no spear, no axe, no bow and arrow (my attempt to rule out anger).

As I was preparing to make my second trip to New Guinea I knew that even if I obtained strong results supporting universality I would need to explain why so many smart people, travelers, anthropologists such as Karl Heider, Margaret Mead, Ray Birdwhistell, and many others, had come to believe that expressions were culture specific. I came up with the formulation that this is due to the operation of what I termed *display rules*, rules we learn in the course of growing up about who can show which emotion to whom, and when. Display rules can specify that an emotional expression be suppressed, de-amplified, exaggerated, or masked. Display rules as I formulated the concept operate primarily in public, not in private. So expressions would appear culturally different, due to display rules, especially when observed by outsiders in social situations. Mead and Darwin could both be right!

The idea that it is possible to control facial expression wasn't original with me, but it had not been elaborated before, nor had it been used to explain how and when expressions of emotion would be pan-cultural or culture-specific. The first step in a series of experiments I did in Japan on this topic was facilitated by Dick Lazarus. Dick had spent a sabbatical year at Waseda University and was continuing to do research on stress, comparing Japanese and U.S. college students, measuring their physiological reactions when watching very unpleasant films. I planned to videotape the facial expressions of both Japanese and American students when alone and when in the presence of an authority figure, expecting to find similar expressions when alone, but different facial expressions—due to display rules—in the presence of an authority figure.

First, I had to be certain that Lazarus's unpleasant films called forth facial expressions of any kind in both cultures. I added some pleasant films of nature and of a puppy playing with a flower that I had made. I asked Ned Opton, then a research associate working for Lazarus, if he could show these films to the Japanese college students, recording their facial expressions with a hidden video camera I lent him. He did that very large favor for me on his next trip to Japan to assist Lazarus, but when I looked at the video recordings the angle seemed odd. When I asked about it, Ned told me that there wasn't enough light in the room in which he showed the films, and unable to install better lighting, he instead put a table under the light and had the subjects climb up on the table to watch the films while seated in this odd location.

I now had to show the films to students in America. If I didn't have them also climb up and sit in a chair on top of a table to watch the films, and their expressions were to differ from the Japanese, I wouldn't know if it was culture or not sitting on top of a table to watch the films that generated any difference. So, rather than starting all over and bringing lighting equipment to Japan and recording Japanese students in a normal seating arrangement, I used the strange seating arrangement for the Americans who watched the films. I often thought of this as good example of being trapped by an initial mistake, forced to either start over (the better choice) or persist in making the initial mistake again and again. Impatient as always, I had the students climb up on the table to watch the films.

The studies I then did confirmed that the subjects in both cultures appeared to display a variety of facial expressions related to fear and disgust when watching the Lazarus films, and smiling when watching my nature and puppy films. Now I was ready to do the experiment that I hoped would explain why smart people such as Birdwhistell and Mead had become convinced that facial expressions were culture-specific. My explanation was that they had only seen expressions in public when the people they observed had applied display rules to disguise or otherwise alter the underlying universal facial expressions. My task was to prove that could occur.

In the fall of 1968, I made the arrangements to stop in Japan for six weeks to run the display rules experiment, before going on to New Guinea. I brought with me Sony video recorders (made in Japan but recording on U.S. sixty cycle video speed. I could not use video cameras available in Japan, as they recorded on fifty cycles and would not play once back in America on American video recorders). Upon my arrival at Narita airport outside of Tokyo, my video equipment was seized by Japanese customs.

My host at Waseda University where I was to run this experiment, Professor Tomita, told me I would have to go to the customs office and seek the release of my equipment. I hired an agent to talk to the customs officials, who, as descendants of Samurai, were very independent and would not be likely to talk directly to an American. I spent every day for the next three weeks sitting outside the customs office, while my agent tried to negotiate the release of the video equipment.

I couldn't believe it. Why would they think I would try to sell Japanese-made equipment that would not play Japanese videos, in Tokyo? But they were stubborn; only yielding when a $5000 bond was posted, to be returned when I took the Sony equipment out of Tokyo.

Having wasted most of the time I had allotted to do the study sitting outside the customs office, I only had two weeks to run the display rule experiment. I literally worked night and day, video recording the Japanese students' facial expressions when they were alone and when they were in the presence of a scientist. Later, the same conditions were arranged in Berkeley. Importantly, the students in both countries did not know that my hidden video camera was observing their expressions.

The measurements we made of the facial expressions revealed no difference between the Japanese and Americans when they watched the emotionally arousing films in private. When a scientist was present while they watched the emotionally arousing films, the Japanese but not the Americans masked disgust and fear expressions with a smile. In this one study, I had shown both Darwin's evolved, universal facial expressions (when the students thought they were alone), and Mead's culture-specific expressions (when there was a scientist present) due to the operation of display rules!

For the return trip to New Guinea in 1968 I had invited Neville Hoffman, who had been the public health doctor in the Fore area, and his wife to join me. Having spent two years in New Guinea they were fluent in Pidgin, and well liked by the people. I also asked Wally Friesen, my co-worker, and my then wife Diana, to come as well. We set up our base in Wanitabe. The people were very excited about my return, welcoming me very warmly. The blank audiotapes I had left behind had been woven into jewelry, proudly worn by many of those we encountered. Diana and Neville's wife conducted the experiment with the women, while Wally and I tested the men, with Neville roaming around to answer any questions or uncertainties. Very few arose. The task was easy for them to grasp, quickly performed. By the time we had tested everyone in Wanitabe, the word had spread, and hundreds of people came to us, eager to get the rewards—cigarettes or soap—for such little effort.

The task was simple: reading a short sentence to the person viewing the photographs (such as "he is about to fight"), showing three photographs—for example, one showing what other cultures had judged to be fearful, another depicting what we thought showed sadness, and another showing anger. The person who heard the story (the informant) had to simply point to the expression that fit the story.

I took special care that the person administering the task could not unwittingly influence the informant's selection of which picture fit the story. The person administering the task could not see which three pictures were shown on each trial, just noting whether the informant pointed to the left, right, or middle picture. To decrease the chance that they might learn that the left picture was always being chosen for the story about the child dying, for example, and by that means come to expect that response, I switched around the pictures at the end of each day. All of this was to prevent the person giving the test from unwittingly influencing the informant's selection of which picture fit the story.

In a fairly short time we tested nearly 5 percent of the South Fore, far more than we needed to do a rigorous statistical analysis. The results were very strong for anger, disgust, sadness, and enjoyment. While the fear and surprise faces were not chosen, when the stories for anger, disgust, sadness, or enjoyment stories were read, they were not differentiated from each other. Either photographs judged to be fear or surprise in literate cultures were equally likely to be chosen for a fear or a surprise story.

The findings for anger, disgust, sadness, and happiness were very strong. It didn't matter whether our informants had seen Westerners, magazines, or photographs. The results were the same. We obtained the same results for males and females, for children under ten as for the adults. It was a triumph; I had solved the problem that had been so frustrating the year before.

I also asked some of the South Fore to show me what their face would look like if they were the people in the stories that we read to them. Later when we showed the films I had made of the poses of the South Fore to college students in San Francisco, they had no trouble identifying the fear, anger, sadness, or enjoyment poses. They did just as well as they did in identifying Caucasian examples of these emotions, even though they knew nothing about the South Fore. But fear and surprise expressions were mixed up. Despite this one limitation, the results were very strong, further confirming the results when the South Fore had interpreted the poses of Caucasians.

On this trip I brought portable video equipment with me, recording spontaneous social behavior much like I had seen in the first year study. The difference was that I could inspect what I had recorded each night. When it came time to leave I faced a dilemma about whether to show them the video I had taken of them. I knew some anthropologists would think I shouldn't show it, for that might cause them to become self-conscious about being recorded by cameras. On the other hand, why should I make the decision for them? I decided to show them a few minutes and then ask them if they wanted to see more. They did. They were fascinated. For a number of nights everyone in the village gathered around to watch my videotapes. Immediately their behavior in the village changed. When I walked through with my camera everyone would pose for me, knowing they would be seen that night.

My wife Diana's roommate, when she had been at Harvard, was the then young psychologist Eleanor Rosch, who was married at that time to the anthropologist Karl Heider. Diana told Eleanor about our findings on universals, and Eleanor told Karl, who had worked for a few years in West Irian (Western New Guinea) before marrying Eleanor. Karl was studying the Dani, a culture shown in the documentary film *Gardens of War*, made by Robert Gardner. Heider wrote me that he didn't believe my findings since the Dani don't even have words for emotion. Knowing that he and Eleanor were about to go back to the Dani, I offered to teach him how to administer our expression-story task and to supply him with the materials if he would stop in San Francisco on his way. Nothing better than to have someone convinced you are wrong repeat your study. If they get the same results it enormously strengthens the reliability of your findings. The Dani were quite isolated at the time.

To his surprise, but my delight, Heider's findings with the Dani perfectly replicated what I had found with the South Fore, even to the failure to differentiate fear and surprise. When Margaret Mead attacked my work in New Guinea as an example of the "appalling state of the social sciences," she conveniently ignored Heider's findings, although they were published, as well as our findings on the Fore poses being understood by Americans. Later, I was to find that others didn't care about our results, convinced the findings must be wrong, because our findings didn't fit their theory. Fortunately they have not been the majority.

This work, the New Guinea studies and the Japan study, was completed by 1968, the findings published in articles and books in the late 1960s and into the 1970s. I did a bit more work trying to establish that contempt is universal, but there were no longer visually isolated cultures available. Later, I describe one more study in an exotic, very different culture on a very different aspect of facial expression.

I found out much later that I had made a mistake about where I published some of the findings. While the New Guinea findings were first published in a prestigious scientific journal,[17] my mistake was to publish the display rule findings in a book, albeit a very prestigious series of yearly books, that only published invited chapters.[18] Choosing that outlet allowed me to explain the findings in detail, elaborate the display rule ideas, and integrate the Japanese-American findings with the New Guinea results. A great chapter, from my viewpoint, but most academic psychologists ignored the display rule study because it had not been published in a refereed scientific journal. I lost!

NUMBER 3 *Strong evidence of universality of some facial expressions of emotion, and why wise observers might think otherwise.*

I edited a book to celebrate the 100th anniversary of the publication of Darwin's *Expression* book, first published in 1872. In addition to reporting my own findings on facial expressions and how they related to Darwin's theory and findings, I invited colleagues to write chapters on expression in other mammals and in children, topics that Darwin had wrote about in his *Expression* book. I also asked Silvan to contribute a chapter summarizing his own theories about emotion and expression. He was so slow in preparing his chapter that the book had to be published in 1973, 101 years after the original publication of Darwin's book. The noted sociologist Erving Goffman later told me that book changed his mind; he no longer subscribed to the view of Ray Birdwhistell.

That book, by means unknown to me, came to the attention of Margaret Mead, who launched a very critical attack on it and on me. The banner headline of her review, "The Appalling State of the Human Sciences," was exemplified by me. (I wondered if she had deliberately chosen the word "appalling" as a joke on my first name.) Here is a quote from her five-page review, published in 1975:

> *The narrowness and discipline-centric nature of the book is a continuing example of the appalling state of the human sciences, when members of each discipline treat their specialized approach as the only approach. . . . Ekman's single-minded research goal—to resolve with absolute certainty (an attitude which we usually do not associate with science, which proceeds by a succession of discarded paradigms) that the expression of some, if not all, of the emotions of which the human face is capable, is innate and universal is outlined in full detail.*

Theory of course does change over time, but not some of the facts. We don't question that the heart pumps blood and that a failure to pump consistently and strongly results in dizziness. This is established fact. I had hoped to establish whether or not there were any universals in expression as a *fact*, allowing for a variety of theories why that might or might not be so.

Mead made it clear that she was offended by my attack on her colleague Birdwhistell. Citing my report that Birdwhistell had no evidence for his claims other than his personal observations, Mead wrote:

> *This is the type of canard which disgraces scientific controversy. . . . By repeating the clichéd criticism that Birdwhistell has become a 'captive of his linguistic model' Ekman is guilty of the most gross misrepresentation, a misrepresentation which has been popularized among psychologists who are more interested in validity and reliability than in what they are actually studying.*

It is worth clarifying what this criticism is really about, for it persists to this day—a fundamental disagreement about what is acceptable as evidence. The dispute about facial expression is a symptom of the different rules of evidence in academic psychology on the one hand, and parts of anthropology and the clinical areas of psychology on the other hand. Birdwhistell had not published, nor had he any material, qualitative or quantitative, to substantiate his claims. They were his personal judgments, based on his reputation for being an acute observer, illustrated by convincing examples. That was sufficient for Mead and for many if not most anthropologists, clinical psychologists, and psychiatrists to this day, but not for experimental psychologists. We require evidence independent of personal observation, evidence substantiated by multiple independent observations and evidence that others could examine, using methods that others could repeat, verifying through replication or disputing if the results previously reported were not repeatable.

I am convinced that even when we try to be objective observers we are selective, filtering what we recognize to support what we expect or already believe. If that is true, and I believe no one is exempt from the danger of such filtering, then observations must be obtained in a way that attempts to minimize bias. A standard safeguard is to obtain multiple independent observations to determine whether different people make the same observations. As I will explain later, that is only the first step; it must be bolstered by physically measuring what the observers are seeing, measuring in a way that cannot be biased. We did that in the study comparing the facial activity shown in Japan and the U.S., when alone and when with another person

One of Mead's acolytes, Alan Lomax Jr., carried her banner when I attempted to give an invited address at the annual meeting of the American Anthropological Association. Full of indignation, Lomax got up from the audience just after I was introduced and loudly shouted that I must not be allowed to speak. My findings concealed a fascist, racist agenda! He succeeded in blocking my talk.

I was impressed that I was being taken so seriously, but confused about the accusation of fascism. As Darwin had emphasized, universals in facial expressions supports the unity of mankind, not racial or group differences. Lomax and Mead made the mistake of believing that recognizing that biology plays a role would support the Nazi claim of biologically based superiority of one group (Aryan) as compared to other groups. Darwin had claimed just the opposite. His findings of universality challenged the racists of his time by showing the *unity* of mankind. My evidence of universality attracted the interest of the Dalai Lama when we met nearly forty years later, because I had shown what all people share.

It was not until I read Mead's autobiography some years later that I understood what had motivated her mistaken reasoning. She explained why she was afraid to acknowledge a role for biology in social behavior. With Nazism on the rise she had decided ". . . that the study of inborn differences would have to wait upon less troubled times."[19] After World War II she recognized the role of biology publicly, at least regarding the differences in the roles of men and women. "It is important to take into consideration the possibility that the biological bases of aggression in the two sexes—in human beings as in other mammals—may differ significantly."[20]

One more comment about Margaret Mead. She had taken the dubious responsibility of serving as editor of one of the many English-language editions of Darwin's *Expression* book, a book with which she strongly disagreed! In her introduction she included pictures of Ray Birdwhistell and heralded his views, which contradicted Darwin, a fact she did not mention in her introduction. By coincidence, not informed choice, it was her edition of Darwin's *Expression* book published by Philosophical Library in 1955, which I bought when I was a first-year graduate student but had not read until I started the cross-cultural research.

Once I had seen the Sorenson and Gajdusek films (Gajdusek did some of the filming himself), I got out a copy of Darwin's *The Expression of the Emotions in Man and Animals*, first published in 1872. What a dynamite title! It was a best-seller in its day, and has never gone out of print to this day. The ideas for this book can be found in his early notebooks, more than forty years before he got around to writing this book.

Darwin had visited many strange, exotic places in his five-year voyage around the world, never understanding the languages or symbolic gestures (emblems), but having no trouble with the facial expressions. If we were all descended from Adam and Eve, we would likely have the same facial expressions. That could be the explanation for universality, not natural selection. But universality did challenge the racists of Darwin's time who claimed that Europeans had descended from more advanced progenitors than Africans. Common descent would be established, Darwin thought, by universality.

I consider Darwin's writings on expression and emotion the founding book of the field of psychology, for he did two psychological experiments. He obtained reports from world travelers of the circumstances in which they had observed different expressions, and showed photographs to others to find out what emotion they saw in the expressions. Each study broke new ground, although flawed by modern scientific standards.[21] Darwin was an experimental psychologist, I believe, and his writings on expression the founding book for the field of psychology. In that book he considered the development of facial expression, expression in other animals, and in the mentally ill. No scientist studying the face to this date has used as many data sources as Darwin did.

In 1994 an editor at Harper Collins London, Philip Gwyne Jones, asked me if I would write a few pages to introduce a new edition of Darwin's *Expression* book. He allowed me to greatly expand my role as editor of the third edition of Darwin's great book. I wrote a fifteen-page introduction attempting to explain why this book was ignored in most of the twentieth century. I inserted over one hundred commentaries from a modern scientific perspective, on what Darwin said about various matters, in his text. I wrote most but not all of them, recruiting nearly a dozen scientists to write about matters raised by Darwin about which I don't have the proper expertise.

I also corrected all the typos that remained in every edition up until this one, changed the orientation from left to right of the illustrations that Darwin cared about but whose instructions to his publisher were ignored until this edition. And, I restored into the text two photographs that Darwin discussed for more than a page but had been dropped by the publisher because the original publisher decided there were too many photographs. I believe Darwin's *Expression* book is the first scientific book in the English language to use photographs.

Shortly before I was to submit to the publisher the final version of the third edition (I had spent four months preparing it, working in the Darwin archives at Cambridge

University and also examining Darwin's personal library at Downe House), I had a dream in which Darwin told me how pleased he was that I was bringing attention back to this book, which had been ignored for so long. (I didn't tell him that most scientists don't know Darwin wrote such a book, even Nobel Prize–winning scientists that I knew didn't know about this book!) But Darwin said, my afterword of one hundred pages was too long for his book, I should put it in my own book. Properly chastised, I followed his request.

The afterword in the third edition of Darwin's *Expression* book, which I cut to fifty pages, discusses the struggle among Bateson, Mead, Birdwhistell, Tomkins, and me about Darwin's contribution on emotion and expression. I explain that I am the only one still alive to tell the story, albeit my version of it. What I cut was a discussion of the difference between a sign and a signal, and how it applies to facial expressions. Although the ideas remain important, I never found a place to publish them. (Briefly, both a sign and a signal are informative to the observer, but only the signal has been shaped over the course of time for effective communication to others. For example, a person gasping for breath is a sign that something is blocking the person's air passage, but it is not a signal of that state.)

My copy of Darwin's *Expression* is now falling apart since I have read and reread it so many times, entering extensive marginal notes on every page. Wally Friesen also read that copy of Darwin's book, adding his marginal notes. So, it is Margaret Mead's edition of Darwin's *Expression* book that I studied so carefully! I think it unseemly of her to have edited a book with which she strongly disagreed, never revealing that to the readers.

I have donated that edition of Darwin's *Expression* book, along with first editions of his original book in 1872, to the rare books library at UCSF.

It was an honor, of benefit for me, still quite an unknown, to be attacked by such a famous person. A few years later I directly replied to Mead's criticisms but not in as much detail as I have here.

Only just now have I realized that the cross-cultural research represented a major shift in who I was examining. In this research I returned to studying normal, not clinical populations. In my first experiment I had studied normal people (if any student choosing to become a psychotherapist can be considered normal) undergoing the stress interviews. The switch to a clinical population in my first grant was motivated by my belief that examining the changes that occurred over the course of inpatient hospitalization represented a natural experiment, where there should be major changes in nonverbal behavior. It offered another, non-manipulative way to sample major changes in emotional status. It would also have the benefit of showing the clinical world that nonverbal behavior was important to consider. By sitting behind the patient, as is still done in classical psychoanalysis to this day, the therapist cannot see the patient's face, the major source for monitoring emotions. Analysts have told me that it doesn't matter; eventually the patient will verbalize whatever is shown on the face. That assertion has never been tested, and I suspect is wrong. Knowing the emotions that are unspoken, which may or may not consciously register in the patient, seems foolish to ignore, without evidence that by ignoring the patient's expressions therapy is more successful or shorter.

There were two more reasons for focusing in my first grant on depressed patients. If memory serves me right, it was the clinical branch of NIMH, which, in 1962, had funding for research. They might have funded basic research on a normal population with the promise that it would yield results that could subsequently be applied to clinical populations, but I did not think that was as certain as a study focused on a clinical population. If I did not succeed in my first grant application, I would not have a second chance; I would have to support myself by doing clinical work or patching together a number of part-time teaching jobs at various state colleges and municipal junior colleges—becoming what is now called a gypsy scholar.

I recognize now, but I didn't then, another motivation: I needed to work with a population of people with afflictions similar to my mother's bipolar disorder. While she did not respond to treatment, I would document how such patients did respond and recovered, at least for a time.

Looked at from a different angle now, I wonder what the best path for discovery of basic knowledge of human nature is, of how emotions work and are shown. Would it be to study the pathological or the normal, if there was a choice and if either could be pursued? Freud developed his theories examining his patients, and presumably observing people in general, but it was his patients that he knew best. There is no doubt in my mind that Freud discovered (or publicized, if you think these ideas existed in some form before him) what are now basic building blocks in our understanding of human nature. Much of our mental life, many if not all of our important evaluations and decisions, occur outside of our awareness. What we are conscious of, our thoughts that we focus upon, are the tip of a very large iceberg. And, no doubt sexual fantasies and desires play an important, not fully recognized, role in our life. Those are two giant discoveries, made by studying a clinical population.

I suspect that many of Freud's other theories such as the Oedipus complex, or the psychosexual stages of development, are not relevant to normal populations, only the clinical ones he studied. But it is beyond my expertise to judge which of Freud's theories is relevant to human nature and which are specific to a particular clinical population, at a specific point in time. I mention it only to document that although major discoveries were made examining clinical populations, I believe that progress in understanding the nature of emotion is best served at this point in time by examining normal not clinical populations. That is what the cross-cultural grant allowed me to do, and what I have continued to do throughout the rest of my career.

CHAPTER 7

How I Became a Tenured Full Professor at UCSF, 1971

THE THEN chairman of the psychiatry department at UCSF, Alexander Simon, told me he was happy to administer my grants and career awards, taking the overhead allotment, but so as long as he was chairman I would never get a faculty position. He would not waste tenure on a psychologist! (He explained that he had given a tenure slot to the psychologist John Starkweather, who absented himself from the department for most of his career to run the campus computer center. No direct benefit to the department; a waste of a tenured slot from Simon's viewpoint.)

When some years later Simon heard that I was visiting Harvard, considering an offer of a faculty position in human relations in the School of Education, Simon had the gall to call me, reaching me during one of my interviews. He wanted to reassure me, he said, that Langley Porter would do nothing to stand in my way from accepting a position at Harvard, adding that it was an honor for me to be so considered.

It was my peace research that got me the tenured faculty position at UCSF, not my findings on expressions and gesture. In 1970, shortly after the invasion of Cambodia, which came to be called the Cambodia Incursion, a very small student radical group handed out flyers calling for a campus-wide meeting to discuss closing the university in protest. I was firmly opposed; fascists closed universities, not supposedly liberal groups. UCSF is a medical center, with responsibilities for patient care, not just teaching and research. All the more reason why closing it would be a mistake, which might alienate even those who opposed the Cambodia Incursion.

I designed a questionnaire about how the citizens of San Francisco would feel if UCSF was closed in protest, mobilized the ABSSOP (Application of Behavioral Sciences to the Strategies of Peace) group of volunteer behavioral scientists, and in less than two days obtained through a telephone survey a random sample of the city. Working all night, we got the data in and out of the computer for analysis. I arrived at the Wednesday campus-wide meeting armed with a few hundred dittoed copies of the report on what we had found.

I waited until the student radical group had made their case for closing the university, and then asked if those attending this meeting wanted to know how the citizens of San Francisco would respond if UCSF was to be closed for even a day. I reported strong opposition, even by those who opposed the Cambodia Incursion. Instead of closing UCSF, I said we should hold a teach-in on the coming weekend, having all-day sessions in which the pros and cons of the Cambodia Incursion would be discussed.

The student radical group said they would participate, but would prevent anyone who supported President Nixon's Cambodia Incursion from speaking.

Chancellor Philip R. Lee announced he was appointing me chief campus officer for the weekend, as he would be out of town. I had never met the chancellor. I was a lowly nonmedical researcher raising my own funding, not in that sense part of the university; it was a marriage of convenience.

When I met Lee shortly before the weekend teach-in, it was for the first time. He said it would be my responsibility to decide whether to call the police to maintain order. I didn't want that responsibility, but Lee impressed me. I knew he had been largely responsible for writing the Medicare legislation under former President Johnson. He was called by many "America's doctor." He was a charismatic person, whom I was eager to get to know better.

At the teach-in I let the people who opposed the Cambodia Incursion speak, not all of whom argued for closing the university. After lunch I introduced an army officer whom I had invited to explain the rationale for the Cambodia Incursion. Some of the protestors got up from their seats, shouting him down. I let it go on for about ten minutes, and then asked the assembled audience if they wanted to listen to the counterargument or not. Fortunately, they overwhelming shouted "yes," shutting up those who were trying to prevent it. I didn't need to call the police.

The very next Monday, Chancellor Lee called me into his office. "Who are you, what do you do?" he asked. Once he heard about my research interests and accomplishments, both on nonverbal behavior and peace research, he said he needed me on his faculty and would appoint me as a full professor. (I have often boasted that I never climbed the academic ladder from assistant to associate to full professor.)

Lee explained to me that the major medical problems of the time could be prevented—smoking, drug abuse, and obesity. Remember this was 1970! What foresight! He planned to open on the campus what he called a School of Human Biology to focus on prevention, and was appointing me the first professor in that yet-to-exist school. A few months later, as we got to know each other better, he asked me if I would be his candidate to be dean of this new school. I agreed; I could not say "no" to anything that Phil (we were now on a first name basis) asked of me.

I got a commitment to continue my research on what I now called Human Interaction and Conflict, a support budget, and another tenured faculty slot that I could fill to join me in my new lab. The dean of the medical school, Julius Krevins, who by virtue of his budget had more clout than the chancellor, did not want another school on the campus, and blocked Phil's plans. Within another year Phil had resigned as chancellor, heading instead a new institute on medical policy.

Krevins, whom I had not before met, called me in for a meeting. He announced that Phil had used a medical school faculty position to appoint me, without his consent. Now Phil was gone, and with no one to protect me, people had their knives out—but he didn't hold a grudge. This was largely bravado. I had the professorship, which Krevins could not take away, and the commitments for my laboratory. We became enemies. Two decades later I sued Krevins, but that story comes later. Krevins did have the power to put my professorship where he wanted it to be located. He stuck me in the psychiatry department and since it was an extra position Chairman Simon did not object.

Phil and I have stayed in touch through the years. At a ceremony to honor his retirement he said the best thing he had done, as chancellor, was to appoint me. What a sweetheart! Although I was administratively located within the psychiatry department, I was not in the Langley Porter building. Instead, I had three adjacent two-story houses that were converted into a laboratory and offices for my staff five blocks away.

In 1967, about the time I was planning my second trip to New Guinea, I was asked by Enoch Calloway, the director of research in the psychiatry department at UCSF, if I would teach his class to the psychiatric residents while he was traveling abroad. I had never before had the opportunity to teach the psychiatry residents—an opportunity usually reserved for those medically trained, not psychologists.

I began by explaining to them the findings I had obtained on the changes in expressions and gestures that marked clinical improvement. After a few minutes they asked me if I had an answer to a problem they confronted. It was up to them whether or not to grant a day or weekend pass to patients who had been hospitalized because of a prior serious suicide attempt. Those who asked for the passes claimed to no longer be having suicidal plans and most of them weren't. But a few were lying, concealing their suicidal plans, in order to complete the act once free of the hospital's supervision. Did I know how they could tell from the patient's behavior whether they were lying?

It raised a fascinating, important set of questions: How convincingly can anyone fabricate emotions they don't feel? And how well can anyone completely hide very strong emotional feelings? I didn't know the answers, but I did know that micro expressions and gestural slips would be relevant. It took twenty-five years to get definitive evidence of how nonverbal behavior can betray very high stakes lies. Like the cross-cultural study, the question wasn't mine. It was given to me. I recognized how important it was, and I ran with it, as hard as I could. Over the next twenty years I created experiments that revealed how signs of emotions felt about engaging in a lie can betray the lie. I describe those experiments later in pages 117–118.

In overlapping time I decided that in order to make progress I needed to be able to compare behaviors that occurred at different points in time during a clinical interview. In order to do so, I needed to be able to do high-speed searches of video recordings and automatically edit onto new videos excerpts I wanted to visually compare. I got a grant to interface, for the first time, computers with video recordings, allowing me to hire Tom Tausig, an engineer, to take on this task. The computer, which was taller than me, had 8K of memory and cost $110,000. We had to communicate with the computer by teletype. After eighteen months of work, we had the first interface between a computer and video recordings, allowing high-speed search and edits. That capability can now, forty years later, be bought for under $5000.

I stopped most of my research while I waited for the computer system (which I dubbed VIDR, "Visual

Information Display and Retrieval"[22]) and instead allowed myself to think about what I had learned and theorize about what lay ahead.

It may seem odd that I had to give myself permission to think, but remember that I was trained in research methods by a Skinnerian, and they had an explicit bias against theory not grounded in direct observation. And, I had managed to get through the period before and after my mother's suicide by not thinking about the risky escapades I knew were occurring in her life that led to her suicide.

Tom Sebeok, the central figure in the last century promoting the field of semiotics, launched a journal, *Semiotica*, and invited me to write an article for the first issue. I didn't know that he had also invited Margaret Mead to write an article. We appeared side by side not directly addressing our disagreements, as neither of us knew the other would be appearing.

My chapter was titled "The Repertoire of Nonverbal Behavior: Categories, Origins, Usage and Coding."[23] I laid out theoretical distinctions among different kinds of nonverbal behavior based on their "origins, usage, and coding," and theorized about each. Published in 1969, this article remains the seminal theoretical description of my approach. I described the differences among three types of bodily movements: *illustrators* (eight ways bodily movement can illustrate speech), *emblems* (symbolic gestures with precise meaning), and *self-adaptors* (in which one part of the body manipulates in some way another body part, which I was later to label manipulators not self-adaptors). I also laid out the time line for the appearance of an emotional expression, including the operation of an affect program and display rules. Much of what I have done in the more than forty years since that publication has been an elaboration of what I wrote then, not a replacement.

While waiting for the computer-video system to be developed, I also wrote my first article about deception: "Nonverbal Leakage and Clues to Deception,[24] which was published in a prestigious journal in 1969. I cited Erving Goffman in the opening paragraph, not knowing that it was Erving who would be asked by the journal to review the paper. I do believe he would have liked the paper even if I hadn't cited him, but I never asked him. In later years, he became a close friend and we spent both work and social time together, which I describe later.

Rereading now that very early paper on deception, I am surprised about how much of it withstands the test of time, and how many ideas are in it that I did not further pursue, although they were, in my judgment today, very much worth pursuing. I became distracted by the task of obtaining evidence of how nonverbal behaviors can betray a lie, even though most people will be blind to the tip-offs. In this very early paper in 1969 I first described *micro facial expressions*, very fast facial expressions that occur when attempts are made deliberately or unconsciously to conceal information. The study of micro expressions and the creation of an online training tool that teaches people how to recognize micros were to occupy much of my time twenty years later. I recognized in this early article the complexity of facial expression: ". . . the face is equipped to lie the most and leak the most, and thus can be a very confusing source of information during deception."

CHAPTER 8

Facial Measurement: FACS, 1972–1978

I HAD ALREADY DEVELOPED and published a tool for measuring facial movements, the Facial Affect Scoring Technique (FAST),[25] which we had used to measure the facial movements shown by the Japanese and American subjects in the display rule study. FAST was based on what we had found in posed facial expressions. A year after it was published, an anthropologist, Wade Seaford, showed me a facial movement on his own face that was not included in FAST. He pushed up his lower lip activating the *mentalis* muscle in his chin area. I was devastated by Wade's demonstration, not knowing how much else, how many other facial movements we had missed in creating FAST. The only way to have a comprehensive system, to include everything the face can and sometimes does do, would be to base it on how the muscles worked to change facial appearance, the anatomy of facial movement. And that is what we did, albeit reluctantly.

Part of my reluctance I trace back now to my wish to avoid any body of knowledge or endeavor that involved medical practice, because of my intense rejection of my cruel physician father. If it had not been for that tortured relationship I might well have ended up as a neurologist, and might not have tackled any of the problems I am known for today. But I had no choice, I knew, if I was to develop a comprehensive system of facial measurement—I would have to learn facial anatomy. I ended up creating a functional anatomy, illustrating in text, photographs, and film, how muscular actions change facial appearance. A topic largely heretofore ignored (with two exceptions I describe below) because there was no medical intervention that required it—you can't fracture your face.

When I told Silvan what I intended to do, he strongly advised me not to attempt it. Facial movements are too complicated to ever thoroughly catalog, let alone measure, he said. He cautioned me that I would get lost and very likely fail. Wally Friesen was also reluctant, but once I started, Wally became thoroughly engaged and was a true partner in developing the Facial Action Coding System, FACS.

My motivation for taking on this daunting task was twofold: I knew we would need a very precise and sensitive facial measurement tool to spot clues to deceit in the face, and I wanted to make it possible for any scientist to extract the information Silvan was able to see in expressions. Also, I had to provide a substitute for FAST, since I now knew it was incomplete. Just how incomplete I could only discover by developing a truly comprehensive measurement system based on the anatomy of facial movement. I had a five-year grant from NIMH to continue my study of depressive patients, and I thought I could justify spending some of that time creating a facial measurement tool, which could then be used to evaluate the depressive patients. I didn't realize when I started that it would take more than the five years to complete, and that I would run out of grant money before I finished.

The standard anatomy textbooks were not of much help. They showed where muscle strands were, but not how the muscles generated changes in facial appearance, the expressions. It was a dead anatomy, constructed from dissections of dead people. We needed a functional anatomy, but it didn't exist, so we had to create it.

Duchenne du Boulogne's book on the mechanics of facial movement was of great use. It had been published in 1862, never translated from the French, and long out of print.[26] (Some years later I arranged for Andrew Cuthbertson's translation into English to be published.[27] Andrew had translated Duchenne's book for his Master's project.) Darwin included some of Duchenne's photographs and findings in his own book. I was to later find some of the correspondence between the two of them. Darwin offered to pay Duchenne for using his photographs, but Duchenne replied that between men of science there should be no financial transactions!

Duchenne, a neurologist living in Paris, worked with some patients who had no pain sensations in their face, so it did not hurt when he electrically stimulated muscle areas on their face, photographing the resulting movement that occurred. So, for example, he put the electrode on the bony area high in the cheek (known as the zygomatic arch), which generated a smiling appearance. This proved that the muscle extending from the zygomatic arch to the lip corners was responsible for a smiling appearance.

By good luck, one of the very few surviving copies of Duchenne's book was in the rare books section of my university's library. A postdoctoral fellow working in my lab, Harriet Oster, who had been a French major as an undergraduate, was my intermediary, describing in detail what Duchenne had found. Duchenne was helpful on the single muscular contractions and the changes in appearance when there were contractions of two muscles simultaneously, but he did not explore all of the two muscle contractions, nor how the simultaneous action of three or more muscles would change appearance, except for one or two exceptions. There were some other limitations in his work, but it was of great help.

Of great importance was his observation that the smile resulting from the contraction of the *zygomatic major* muscle did not appear convincing. That happened only when it was accompanied by the contraction of *orbicularis oculi*, the muscle circling around the eyes. I further refined Duchenne's discovery by isolating it to just one of the two strands of the *orbicularis oculi* muscle, labeled as *pars lateralis* in the anatomy texts. In other research, I found that most people could not voluntarily contract this muscle.

Duchenne said the absence of *orbicularis oculi* "unmasks the false friend," but he did not note that when the *zygomatic major* muscle is strongly contracted, generating a broad smile, it also a produces many of the most obvious signs that are generated by *orbicularis oculi, pars lateralis* (raised cheeks, crow's feet wrinkles) even though that muscle has *not* contracted. One must look for a slight lowering of the eyebrow and the eye cover fold (the skin between the eyebrow and the upper eyelid) as evidence for the genuine smile when the smile is broad. Because this is such a subtle sign I conjecture that it must not have been of much social benefit over the course of our evolution to distinguish genuine from simulated smiles, for if it was, a clear signal would have developed. However, when the smile is slight, then the signs produced by *orbicularis oculi* are not produced by *zygomatic major,* and it is easy to discern whether the smile is genuine or put on. In his honor I have in my writings named the genuine smile generated by *zygomatic major* and *orbicularis oculi, pars lateralis* as the Duchenne smile.

Duchenne's observations about smiling have broader implications for distinguishing voluntary from involuntary expressions. If a muscular action is difficult to perform voluntarily, its absence is a mark that the facial expression is not generated by an emotion. Such difficult-to-perform actions mark what I have called *reliable* facial expressions; in *Emotions Revealed* I have described the reliable sign for fear, anger, surprise, and sadness.

Building upon Duchenne's descriptions for more than a year, Wally and I sat in front of video and still cameras as we tried to make each muscle contract, one by one. It wasn't hard for me to do, for I have always had exceptional control of my facial muscles. My mother often told me not to make all the crazy facial expressions with which I would try to entertain her, warning me they might freeze on my face. She didn't live long enough to find out how that ability helped me in one of my most useful scientific studies.

For every muscle contraction, we wrote a precise description of how it changed facial appearance, highlighting what the video recordings depicted. We identified a little more than forty *Action Units,* or *AUs,* and then examined what occurred when two of the AUs occurred simultaneously. We cataloged more than three hundred AU two-way combinations, and then took on all the combinations of three AUs, and so on, until we stopped at combinations of six AUs. There were a few cases in which we could not be certain which muscle we were voluntarily contracting, so I had a needle inserted into my face to electrically stimulate one or another muscle. It was painful, but we didn't have to do it very often. (I didn't electrically stimulate the surface of the face as Duchenne had done, since the muscles are very close to each other in the regions I was focused upon, necessitating this more precise, but painful, method.)

When we were about halfway through cataloging these various facial combinations, I heard that there was a Swedish anatomist who had generated a functional anatomy of facial expression. I visited Professor Hjorstjo in the anatomy department of the University of Lund, and found that he had indeed just published a book based on using the same method we had adopted, voluntarily contracting single muscles and some combinations and photographing the changes.[28] His book, which was in English, used drawings of the face, based on his photographs. While useful in corroborating our findings to date, it was incomplete and not intended to provide a measurement tool.

By the end of four years we had completed what we intended to be a self-instructional manual, including photographs and filmed examples of each AU and many of the combinations. Now we needed to determine whether it was possible for people to learn from the manual to reliably score facial movements in the same way. I called my program officer at NIMH to see if he would entertain additional funding, but when he found out I had spent the entire current grant to create this tool and had not yet actually measured the behavior of any depressed patients, he turned me down.

I was threatened. A lack of funds would close my laboratory and stop my work just when we were on the verge of providing what has turned out to be a tool used by so many people: actors and acting coaches, scientists, animators, artists, interrogators, advertisers, and many in other fields. We had already learned a lot. We now knew how many different facial expressions a human being can make—about ten thousand. And we had a hunch and some observations that suggested less than three thousand of these possible expressions were related to emotion.

But we had to prove that it worked, that when different people studied the manual and then scored facial movements (which we were to provide) they would come up with the same scoring. It would take more than a year to create the video examples to be scored by learners, and it would take six months to recruit a group to learn FACS, and then test their ability. But I didn't have the money to do it.

Out of the blue I got a phone call from a fellow who identified himself as Lionel Tiger. He said that he and his colleague Robin Fox were the co-directors of the Harry Frank Guggenheim foundation, the little one, not the big

Solomon Guggenheim foundation. They liked my work, he said, and wanted to know if I needed any funding. I thought it was a joke. Tiger and Fox calling, offering money! I asked the caller to stop "pulling my leg." He convinced me that they were really who they said they were, inviting me to meet them at their hotel for a drink. I did, and they gave me the funds for the next two years to complete the FACS test of reliability.

Three postdoctoral fellows in my lab at that time, Linda Camras, Harriet Oster, and Rainer Krause; one pre-doctoral fellow, Charlotte Baker; and two research assistants comprised the group who would determine if FACS was reliable. We gave each of them a copy of the FACS manual and the video they were to score when they had finished studying the manual. I remember, as do they, what I said to them when they were about to begin. It was something like this:

> *You must each learn FACS separately, and not talk to each other. And you must each separately score the Final Test video, and again not talk to each other. We don't know if FACS is going to work, if you are going to score the Final Test in the same way. If you do, we will publish it and others will then be able to use it. If you do not score it the same way we will try to figure out why and if we can fix it. You must work as hard as you can; if we were to fail because you didn't try hard, that would be a tragedy. In some sense, the fate of facial measurement is in your hands. Do your very best!*

They did. And it was reliable. FACS was published in 1978,[29] and more than one thousand scientists and many more graduate students have used FACS in their research.

A volume[30] has been published reprinting some of their published scientific articles using FACS. Animation studios, such as Pixar, Disney, and Industrial Light and Magic, have all studied FACS.

NUMBER 4 The creation of a method for comprehensively and objectively measuring facial movement: FACS.

To accomplish a complete FACS measurement of one minute of facial behavior—which means identifying each Action Unit (AU) (and often there are a few AUs generating an expression), exactly when it began to appear, when it reached its apex, how long the apex was held on the face, when it began to decline, and when it disappeared—is very slow, precise work. Rarely does just one AU appear. Instead, three to five AUs may appear in overlapping time, creating the impression of an "expression." Usually it takes fifty to sixty minutes to score one minute. Learning FACS is also a slow process requiring seventy-five to one hundred hours, and then a Final Test, which we provide to determine if you have learned it accurately. Nevertheless, in the nearly forty years since FACS was published in 1978, hundreds of articles by various scientists have been published. A selection of them appeared in a volume I co-edited with Erika Rosenberg, *What the Face Reveals*, and a second edition in 2005.

I hoped that it might be possible to have a computer speed up the process, aiding the FACS scorer even if it could not do the whole job. My friend Bob Levenson (whom I write more about more when I discuss how we discovered that making faces turns on our emotions) warned that would be a disaster. Indeed, only the most serious dedicated scientists use FACS, because it took a lot of work. If it could be done quickly, then hordes of slipshod scientists, who abound in academic psychology, would do slipshod research on the face. I didn't do anything actively to find a computer-driven FACS; I stumbled upon one.

After giving a paper at a conference in Wales on the face, I heard a computer scientist working for the British government describe the system he had developed for facial recognition. (I prefer to use the term *Identity recognition*, "who are you?" contrasting that with *Emotion recognition*, "what are you feeling?" But the computer science world continues to use the phrase *face recognition*, not specific enough in my judgment to make it clear which question is being asked.) Using neural networks with a computer he had built that was capable of parallel processing;, he had taught it to recognize twenty-five different people, automatically. (He had also taught his system how to recognize the profiles of tanks from unfriendly countries.) The computer could spot problematic people who might be approaching a secure facility from fifty feet away. The only problem, he said, was when someone made a facial expression; it often changed their appearance so much that the computer couldn't recognize who the person was.

I talked with him after his presentation, telling him that his noise—facial movements—was my data, while his data—different facial appearances—was my noise. He invited me to visit his lab at Brunel College outside London and use his computer to see how it would work for my task. I was on sabbatical in London at the time, and spent four days using his computer, which he had named the Wizard. By showing the Wizard repeated examples of each of three forehead movements—brows lowered (AU4), inner and outer portions of the eyebrows raised (AU1 + AU2), and eyebrows angling upwards in the center (AU1 + AU4)—the Wizard learned in a few days to recognize which AUs were occurring when I brought a variety of different people in front of the input camera and told them to make one of those three movements. If I could train the Wizard to recognize the most frequently occurring AUs, it would save an investigator at least 70 percent of the time it takes to use FACS.

I wrote a grant proposal to NIMH to do just that. It was rejected. The reviewers wrote that computers can't do what I had proposed, that I was mistaken. The proposal had been reviewed by people who did not know the cutting edge of computer science. But Terry Sejnowski did.

Terry is to neural nets what I am to faces. If I had known him, I would have recruited him to be on my proposal. He was a friend of a friend of mine, the late Don Glaser, a Nobel Prize winner with a keen and playful mind. I had lamented to Don one day over dinner about the fate of my project to automate facial measurement. Don told his friend Terry about what I was trying to do, Terry asked to see my grant proposal, said it could be done, and we jointly wrote a grant proposal to the National Science Foundation (NSF), where it was reviewed by a panel knowledgeable about neural nets and parallel processing computers. We got the grant; Marni Bartlett, a student of Terry's, did all the work; I supplied the exemplars of each AU the net learned to spot. Our success was published in

1996 and 1999. I moved into the back seat, for the real work was on the computer side. I was only providing the exemplars needed to train the net.

Nonetheless, I was getting known in the computer or IT world, which led NSF to ask me to organize an international conference on automating facial measurement, which I did. About thirty people from Europe, the Americas, and Asia attended; all were just beginning to approach the problem. I had learned by then that the main alternative to the neural net approach to accomplish this task was AI (artificial intelligence). I recruited onto the planning committee for the conference a highly regarded AI person interested in the face, Takeo Kanade, to join Terry Sejnowski and me. The conference was a success.

CHAPTER 9

The Horse Race

I CAN'T REMEMBER how I learned that the CIA was interested in automating facial measurement, assigning this task to Rowena Swanson. I had by then some credentials with the CIA from my work on deception, and I had been asked to brief senior officials more than once. I remember one such briefing when I was told that everyone in that room knew a lot about me, but I could not know their names, only hear their questions. They were good questions.

I was never asked anything that implied or bordered on something that I as a liberal, left democrat considered unethical. I was not and am not against the existence of the CIA. I believe any industrialized country needs espionage, and counterespionage, and very good intelligence. I was most concerned that the CIA, part of the Department of Defense, and the FBI were being oversold by psychiatrists and marginal scientists who claimed they could always tell when someone was lying. I was not impressed by the experts they were relying upon.

I was invited to talk to the Israeli National Police more than once; the last time was when they had a government with which I was sympathetic. I mention it because in Israel the top scientists work with the police; in the United States, with a few exceptions, it is the reverse.

I convinced the CIA that we needed to have a horse race in which I would supply the fodder (carefully FACS-scored videos of people lying or telling the truth). There would be two horses in the race (the neural net Sejnowski-Bartlett team and the Jeff Cohn and Takeo Kanade AI team). The referees who would evaluate progress every three months would be agreed to ahead of time by the horses. The CIA lady Rowena Swanson bought it, I organized it, and we had a meeting in which everyone got to know each other, and then they were off to the races! After three and six months we had evaluations by the referees; the estimates were that it would take about two years for the first round of the race. Depending on the race outcome and referee recommendations, more races would occur with different fodder, building on experience from the first race. Even though I was not doing the work, I was the hand behind the curtain, as I had organized it. This is how science should operate. It is the only way to know whether two alternative measurement procedures yield the same or different things.

And then the Witch came in, as Nora Slatkin came to be known. She was the new executive director of the CIA under John M. Deutsch, the director appointed by President Bill Clinton in 1995. I was told the Witch said, "Don't you have anything better to spend money on?" canceling the horse race. The horses went their own way, each developing a usable automated facial measurement procedure. I have been trying to convince them to resurrect the horse race, so the scientific community can learn what the possible overlap is, which works best for answering which questions, with which kinds of videos. I suspect I won't succeed.

I was a minority shareholder in one of these companies involved in the horse race, Emotient Inc. In some sense I'm a founder and chair of their Scientific Advisory Board, which has never asked me for advice. I liked the people who are doing it. Marni remained a main figure on the science side, but an investor has taken control and appointed his own CEO. This would all be to the good, depending on how they use their new capabilities. One of their projects analyzes the emotional reactions of customers in a supermarket as they look at different products or ads. I have taken issue with this in a recent interview in the *Wall Street Journal*, from which I quote:

Using Psychology and Data Mining to Discern Emotions as People Shop, Watch Ads; Breeding Privacy Concerns"

Companies are amassing an enormous database of human emotions, using technology that relies on algorithms to analyze people's faces and potentially discover their deepest feelings. While the evolving technology has many potential benefits, it's also raising privacy concerns.

Paul Ekman, perhaps the world's most famous face reader, fears he has created a monster. . . . Now, a group of young companies with names like Emotient Inc., Affectiva Inc., and Eyeris are using Dr. Ekman's research as the backbone of a technology that relies on algorithms to analyze people's faces and potentially discover their deepest feelings. Collectively, they are amassing an enormous visual database of human emotions, seeking patterns that can predict emotional reactions and behavior on a massive scale.

Dr. Ekman, who agreed to become an adviser to Emotient, says he is torn between the potential power of all this data and the need to ensure it is used responsibly, without infringing on personal privacy.

So far, the technology has been used mostly for market research. Emotient, a San Diego startup whose software can recognize emotions from a database of micro expressions that happen in a fraction of a second, has worked with Honda Motor Co. and Procter & Gamble Co. to gauge people's emotions as they try out products. Affectiva, an emotion-detection software maker based in Waltham, Mass., has used webcams to monitor consumers as they watch ads for companies like Coca-Cola Co. and Unilever PLC.

The evolving technology has the potential to help people or even save lives. Cameras that could sense when a trucker is exhausted might prevent him from falling asleep at the wheel. Putting cameras embedded with emotion sensing software in the classroom could help teachers determine whether they were holding their students' attention.

But other applications are likely to breed privacy concerns. One retailer, for instance, is starting to test software embedded in security cameras that can scan people's faces and divine their emotions as they walk in and out of its stores. Eyeris, based in Mountain View, Calif., says it has sold its software to federal law-enforcement agencies for use in interrogations.

The danger, Dr. Ekman and privacy advocates say, is that the technology could reveal people's emotions without their consent, and their feelings could be misinterpreted. People might try to use the software to determine whether their spouse was lying, police might read the emotions of crowds, or employers might use it to secretly monitor workers or job applicants.

"I can't control usage," Dr. Ekman says. . . . "I can only be certain that what I'm providing is at least an accurate depiction of when someone is concealing emotion."

An unidentified retailer is using Emotient's software in its security cameras to gauge whether shoppers are pleased when looking at products and leaving the store.

As with many other technologies, emotion-detection software raises all sorts of privacy questions. "I can see few things more invasive than trying to record someone's emotions in a database," said Ginger McCall, a privacy advocate.

In the mid-2000s, former detective Charles Lieberman trained detectives in the New York Police Department's counterterrorism unit in Dr. Ekman's facial-coding system. He said the technology could help interrogators if they could identify inconsistencies between a suspect's story and emotions revealed on his or her face. But, he cautioned, it is important to "recognize its limitations—it can lead you in the right direction but is not definitive."

Problems could also arise if the software isn't perfectly accurate. Emotions, such as sadness or frustration, could be wrongly interpreted. People could be wrongly pegged as liars. Emotient claims its software is highly accurate, but the accuracy of the system hasn't been independently tested.

With no regulation, the companies are writing the privacy rules as they go.

Ken Denman, CEO of Emotient, says his company makes a point of discarding the images of individual faces within seconds after it has logged the sentiment they express. "There's very little value in the facial expression of any individual," he said.

. . . Dr. Ekman says he hopes the government will step in and write rules to protect people. He says that in public spaces, such as shopping malls, consumers should at least be informed if their emotions are captured.

Apple recently bought Emotient but won't reveal what it is doing with it.

In academia, federal rules require that anyone doing research with human subjects must have their proposal reviewed by an independent body of scientists; the people who will be studied must be notified, and their consent given for that use. That is missing from what companies such as Emotient and Apple are doing.

Emotient claims there is no problem because they don't keep the analyses of individual facial expressions and don't link it to individual persons. How do we know that is true, or that other users of Emotient do the same, or that their competitors follow the same rules? I strongly believe that if you are in a public place, such as a supermarket, your emotional reactions should remain private unless, at a minimum, there are signs informing you that your emotional reactions may be measured. If this becomes unavoidable, the only way to have privacy and not have people record your emotional reactions without your knowledge—the only way to escape such a Frankenstein monster invading your privacy—will be to wear masks in public! Equally frightening—people may not care. Exhibitionism will have a new arena!

To calm the prose down a bit, although I choose not to inhibit my report of how strongly I feel about this, let me quote from a dream of the future I published in 1987 about what might someday be possible:

> *The last item on the standardized intake questionnaire tells Ms. R to turn on the TV set and put on the headphones. A series of six one-minute films, each evoking a different emotion, appears on the screen. . . . The video camera mounted in the video monitor transmits her facial expressions to a automated facial real-time analyzer, [such as Emotient], providing the doctor a profile of the strength of each of her emotions.*

This benevolent use of automated facial measurement could help the physician or nurse monitor changes in the patient's emotional repertoire, making suitable adjustments to the treatment being offered. But it would be done with informed consent!

Let me change the topic. To my great delight, a group of scientists in Plymouth, England, created ChimpFACS. They knew, as did I, that the same muscles are found in the chimp and human face, but the faces sometimes appear to generate different expressions because they pull the skin over different bony structures, typically also with different amounts of hair growing on that skin. With Chimp-FACS it is now possible to directly compare human and chimpanzee facial expressions in similar social contexts! It would have pleased Darwin; it certainly pleased me!

CHAPTER 10

Catching People Lying about Suicidal Plans

WHILE DEVELOPING FACS, I also launched my first set of experiments to discover how well we could uncover lies. I tried to design an experiment that would have applicability to the concern of the psychiatric residents who had to decide if patients were lying about whether they intended to commit suicide if given a weekend pass from the hospital. The subjects in my experiments would have to be as highly motivated to succeed in their lies as the deceptive suicidal patients; their lies would have to involve the concealment of strong negative emotions and the simulation of slight to moderate good cheer. In what became known as the Nurses Study, we did just that.

I convinced the dean of the UCSF School of Nursing that her students could learn how to regulate their emotions by participating in my experiment. She wrote a letter to incoming students describing the possible benefits if they were to participate. One hundred percent of them did. We told them that often in nursing practice they would witness suffering, or gore, and have to conceal their feelings. Our experiment would give them practice in developing the necessary skills. We would show them films of the worst gore they might ever encounter, instructing them to conceal any emotions they felt in response, and describe seeing a pleasant nature film. We also showed them nature films instructing them to describe their feelings honestly. Five of approximately forty nurses broke down in the middle of the five-minute deceptive session, unable to maintain the lie.

Measuring facial expression with FACS, and their hand movements with my classification of illustrators, emblems and self-manipulators, I obtained support for many of my hypotheses about the specific behaviors that betray lying. Those results and my theory about why people lie and what determines whether lies succeed or fail are described in my book *Telling Lies*,[31] first published in 1985 and now in its fourth edition, with new chapters updating the book in each edition. There are translations of this book in many languages.

I had heard that consultants who were claiming they could detect lies were paid by the intelligence agencies in our country and by the KGB in the U.S.S.R. I hoped that *Telling Lies* would show how hard it is to catch liars, even though it is possible in most instances if you analyze the fine details of behavior. *Telling Lies* includes an entire chapter on cautions. It remains my most popular book, and second in my favorites (the number one favorite is *Emotions Revealed*,[32] published in 2003, described later).

I did another series of experiments in which I showed one minute of the nurses' behavior to various occupational groups, asking them to guess whether each sample they saw was from the honest or deceptive interview. Nearly everyone did terribly, at chance levels. Over time I replicated this finding with psychologists, psychiatrists, lawyers, judges, intelligence agents, social workers, and so on, testing the accuracy of nearly fifteen thousand people. Mental health experts and police officers had more confidence in their capability, which our findings contradicted.

The late Maureen O'Sullivan, a professor of psychology at the University of San Francisco, joined me in this set of studies. We did discover that U.S. Secret Service agents did far better than chance. They were pleased and we were curious as to why, attributing it to the possibility that surveillance for a rare event—an assassin in a crowd—forced them to closely scrutinize the details of behavior. Later we found that those intelligence agents who volunteered to take a day's course I taught on how to catch liars were, before training, better than chance, although not as good as the Secret Service. Those psychologists who were willing to give up two days of income from seeing patients to attend a two-day course I taught were also better than chance when I tested them *before* the course. We published those findings. The first set of findings was entitled *Who Can Catch a Liar*,[33] the second set of findings were published as *A Few Can Catch a Liar*.[34] These findings spawned a theory of why and when people lie, and why lies fail or succeed, described in my book *Telling Lies*.

NUMBER 5 *Although lies can be detected from nonverbal behavior, most people can't do much better than chance.*

These findings spawned a theory of why and when people lie, and why lies fail or succeed.

CHAPTER 11

First Trip to the Soviet Union, 1979

IN 1978, I RECEIVED A POSTCARD from a Soviet psychologist, Marc Lasko, which he had given to an American tourist to mail when he returned to the United States. It read, "you will be receiving an invitation to lecture at Leningrad State University. I hope you will accept." I didn't wonder why Lasko had not mailed the letter directly to me, suspecting that intrigue and indirectness were not unusual. I didn't yet know why that was so in this instance.

A few months later I heard from the Council on Scholars (which administers the Fulbright Exchange Program for the State Department), that I had been requested by name to lecture in Leningrad. What would have been more typical would be a request for a person of a particular discipline, or specialist on a particular topic, not a specific person.

I could be the first Fulbright scholar to teach at Leningrad State. I could go for six months on one of their programs, or for six weeks on another; I chose the latter. I filled out the paperwork and a few weeks later, in May 1979, I arrived in Leningrad.

It was a hot moment in the Cold War. The Soviets had recently invaded Afghanistan, and in response President Jimmy Carter withdrew American participation in the Olympics, which was being hosted that year in Russia. Relations between our two countries were not so difficult when I had been invited and I accepted. But once you specify your arrival date and date of return on your visa application, the Soviets allowed no changes other than cancellation. I was determined to go, and to make contact with dissidents. Sacharov, Orloff, and Schransky were all still in the Gulag. A close friend of mine, Philip Siegelman, ran a one-man organization, SOS, which pressured the Russians to let these men out of the Gulag prisons. While I didn't expect I could reach them, I thought perhaps I could reach and help lesser fish.

Another reason I wanted to go was that I had heard that so-called Russian experts were advising the Soviet intelligence agencies, claiming they could tell whether someone was lying. I wanted to explain how difficult it is to do that even when the person is from the same culture and speaks the same language.

After a thirty-hour flight from San Francisco, changing planes in Helsinki, I was met at the airport by a delegation of psychologists from Leningrad State. They took me to my hotel, a beautifully furnished room with a lovely view of the Neva River. They opened a half dozen bottles of Vodka to toast my arrival. Vodka bottles in Russia are constructed in such a way that they cannot be resealed once opened, an incentive to empty each one, which we did. One by one, members of the welcoming delegation peeled off until the only one left was Marc Lasko, my host who had invited me.

Marc held up a piece of paper on which he had written "the room is bugged." Next the message: "I applied today as a Jew to emigrate." I learned later that applying to emigrate as a Jew almost always resulted in immediate loss of employment and a long wait to be allowed to leave, if at all. Marc figured, as it turned out correctly, that they wouldn't fire him with an American professor there to observe their actions, and perhaps they would let him leave. Unfortunately, the Communist Party officials, who were also overseeing my visit, thought I was in on it from the beginning, and therefore treated me with considerable suspicion.

One of my lectures I titled "Why the KGB shouldn't try to interpret Carter's smile." I hoped the KGB would be in the audience, but was surprised they would be so brazen as to come up onto the stage where I was to give my lecture. Before I began, in front of the audience, they quizzed me about my work. At one point, I asked them what part of the Soviet government they worked for. They replied: "The Electrical Institute." Those sitting in the front row of the audience, who heard this exchange, burst out laughing. I learned from this encounter how to recognize at least some members of the KGB: they smoked better cigarettes than most Russians and were much better dressed.

An overflow audience always attended my lectures, with people literally hanging from the rafters. I never found out if they were interested in me, my topic, or hearing an American speak English. After each lecture there was a reception in a large, very beautiful room from Czarist times. The reception was also very well attended, but only four or five people, the same people after each lecture, came up to talk to me. The second time this happened I suspected that those who talked to me were Party members, or had been cleared to do so, while others were afraid to speak to me without permission.

I attempted to overcome this by announcing loudly at the end of the reception that I did not need an escort back to the hotel, but instead would make use of the marvelous Soviet trolley system and go back to the hotel on my own. As I had hoped, soon after I boarded the jam-packed trolley, I heard a voice whisper into my ear, "Dr. Ekman, are you interested in a private meeting?" When I replied, "yes," I was asked for the number of my room, for with that knowledge an outsider could directly call someone in the hotel, a chink in the otherwise firm Soviet system of controlling access to foreigners. I was told while still on the trolley that I should wait in my hotel room for further instructions. I never did see who was whispering in my ear.

A phone call soon after I got to my room instructed me to dress unobtrusively and go to the northwest corner of the block on which the hotel was situated, and wait to be picked up by a taxi. I was not to say a word once in the taxi or on the subways that we would also ride. That is what happened; two taxi rides with subways in between before we arrived at the home of a senior Jewish psychologist who was willing to take the risk of such a secret meeting. His living room was filled with graduate psychology students, who asked me about psychology, never about political matters. We held three other such meetings. Four of those students have become lifelong friends—two immigrated, one to Paris, another to London.

The next day a man named Vladimir Trusov (which I found out means coward in Russian), a psychologist who headed the International Department, responsible for international matters, asked for a meeting. I had been warned that he was a very active Party member, which he never tried to conceal. He asked where I had been the previous night, noting I had come back late to my room. I figured out that one of the women who sat twenty-four hours a day at the end of the hotel hallway reported on me. I told Trusov I had met with a group of students at someone's house. He wanted to know whose house and the names of the students who were there. I told him that I couldn't remember: "Russian names sound alike to an American."

He urged me not to make his job hard. He had to report on me every day, as he was certain I would have to do to the corresponding people in my country. (I was never queried at either the American Consulate in Leningrad or once home, never asked anything about whom I met or what I learned. I am not certain whether or not I think it was a good thing for our country not to care, for I thought then that I had identified a covert KGB agent who would be seeking to emigrate to the U.S. as a so-called "sleeper.")

Trusov cautioned me that America was making a great mistake. The real enemy of both of us was China. We might have more cars, but in Russia they had many more tanks. They were prepared for the inevitable Chinese onslaught; we weren't. There were serious risks to him and to the university by hosting me, and I must be cautious what I did and not be uncooperative. When the American Consulate had a party in my honor, inviting all the members of the university's psychology department, only Lasko showed up. The rest had been told not to go.

After my grilling by Trusov, I told the students at our next meeting what had happened. Only one of them asked me to tell Trusov his name. He had the right, he said, to talk to anyone he chose. This young psychologist was to later become an advisor to Gorbachov.

I was asked if I wanted to meet with the former head of the Bechterov Institute, a neurology treatment and research center, who had been fired when he applied as a Jew to emigrate. He wanted to meet with me, hoping it might help him get permission to leave, as it had been many months since he was fired and he was in limbo. Again we went by taxis and subways to his home. The first thing he did was to put his telephone in the bathroom and close the door, so, he said, the KGB could not hear what we were saying. I thought he was a bit paranoid, only to learn later that most sophisticated intelligence agencies, including our own, can listen to what you say through your landline or cell phone, when you think it is off! Turned off phones can act as a microphone, without your knowledge! He was right; not paranoid.

We talked for a few hours, and I promised I would talk to neurologists in the U.S. about his status, since his research was known in America. He later asked me to come a second time, this time leaving the phone out, betting that they might let him go if an American professor knew about his plight. A few months after I returned to America, he was granted permission to emigrate and obtained a job at one of the VA hospitals.

I asked to visit the shetls where my grandparents came from in what is now called Belorussia. My request was denied, as was my request to visit Talinin in Estonia. Instead I was told I would give lectures in Moscow and then in Kiev. A reasonably comfortable overnight train trip took me to Moscow, where I was hosted by a young female graduate student in the psychology department at Moscow University, one of the many Mashas I met in Russia (as popular a name as Mary in America). She was a lovely young woman, who spoke excellent English, acting as my translator for my lectures.

I found line-by-line translations a very enjoyable method of delivery. I would make a short statement, and then during the pause while it was translated I could process how the listeners were reacting, watching their faces closely. I would take account of whether they seemed to understand or disagree, or whether they were perplexed, bored, or intrigued, as I framed my next short statement.

Over the weekend Masha took me to her family's lovely dacha in the countryside near Moscow, where I met, briefly, her father, reputedly the "father of the Soviet H-bomb." It was because of his importance, Masha proudly told me, that they did not have to be Party members to enjoy access to benefits. In Moscow they had the only apartment I ever saw in Russia that would be acceptable to upper-middle-class Americans.

Anti-Semitism, while officially forbidden, was just below the surface. Since Jews were no more than 1 percent of the Soviet Union's population, they could not be more than 1 percent of the university students—Soviet Affirmative Action. In the identity papers that all Soviets had to carry, it would not say Russian if you were Jewish: even if the last six generations of your family had lived in Russia, the papers would read Jewish. The best-known Soviet psychologist was Lev Vekker. His colleagues were proud that someone from Leningrad State University was known in the West; still, he was a Jew, not a Russian. Imagine if only Christians had birth certificates as Americans!

Over time I was increasingly angry about what I saw and experienced. As a Fulbright scholar I had diplomatic status, which enabled me to shop in *coupon* stores, as they were known, which made no attempt to hide from the Russians who were denied entry unless they were Party members. Those stores were well stocked with Gordon's Gin, Johnny Walker Black scotch, butter, all kinds of other goodies not elsewhere available, and at low prices.

When I asked to visit a museum, it was then closed to the public so I could have it to myself undisturbed. There was a very long line to see Lenin's tomb. Ordinary Russians would have to wait hours to get in. I was taken to the head of the line. And no one in this supposedly class-less society complained about this class discrimination.

They knew how to keep the masses malleable. Trucks dispensed beer every morning, so workers could imbibe before going to work. Another trick was to make food supplies, always in short supply, available in separate lines. First you stood for an hour or more in line for bread, then in another long line for milk, then another for cheese, and so on.

It was aggravating to this American! The longer I spent in Russia the more outraged I became. Fortunately I was scheduled to leave before I started expressing my frustrations.

Marc asked me if I would carry out his dissertation, which he would not be allowed to take if he was ever granted the right to emigrate. Since his dissertation training had been paid for by the Soviet State, the state, not he, owned his dissertation. I thought this so unreasonable that I agreed, knowing I would have to smuggle his dissertation, and if I were to be searched on my departure, there was no way to know in advance what the reaction by the officials might be. He also asked me to take a small painting he had done. I agreed to that also. I wasn't searched.

CHAPTER 12

Return Trip to the Soviet Union, 1990

IT MAY BE SURPRISING that having had such a negative reaction to the Soviet Union during my first trip I went back, only eleven years later, for a second visit. I had two reasons for doing so. I wanted to inoculate my five-year-old-daughter, Eve, and my twelve-year-old-stepson Tom, against the idealization of communism so endemic in academia, by seeing what a communist state was actually like. I went so far as to arrange for both of them to live with Trusov in his apartment, so they would get a full dose of it. My wife, Mary Ann, and I would see them every day, but they ate breakfast and lunch with the Trusovs, saw what I told them was a privileged Soviet apartment, enduring Soviet hallways, which, because they were common space belonging to no one, were filthy and smelly.

Eve developed hives within a day of entering Russia, which disappeared only when she left. A few months after returning from Russia I was invited to lecture in Tuscany. When Mary Ann could not come with me because of other obligations, I asked Eve to join me. She first asked me, "Is it a communist country, Dad?" I knew I had accomplished my purpose.

My second reason for returning to the Soviet Union was to help get one of five political prisoners still in the Gulag freed. My friend Philip Siegelman, who still ran SOS, even though the people whose names had provided those initials—Sakharov, Orlov, and Schransky—were now free, had told me that one scientist, a Jewish physicist named Mischa Kazachakov, remained in the Gulag, a fact little known during the West's enchantment with Gorbachev. Phil gave me a shortwave radio to smuggle in to give to Mischa's mother, who had asked for one. Phil asked me to meet with her and with her son's colleagues at the physics institute from which he had been arrested in the 1970s. If possible I was to videotape interviews with Mrs. K. and members of her son's physics institute.

I quote from the diary I kept on this topic:

Saturday Sasha Etkind [one of the students I came to know in my 1979 visit, who has since emigrated to the West] took me to find Mrs. K. Many apartments are spread out in a nonsystematic way, so that knowing the apartment number does not help you figure out where it might be in this two-block-long massive set of buildings. Mrs. K. lives in a small room, with shared kitchen and toilet, surrounded by her precious art collection. Every wall is covered with paintings, some very good, all very valuable. And in the center is this tiny, seventy-eight years old, woman who looks no more than sixty. She took for granted American interest in her son Mischa. She was gracious and grateful, and when our two hours of conversation ended she seemed very tired. When she spoke of her fears that her son may go on another hunger strike she became tearful.

The KGB won't capitulate [free] Mischa, she said. Why, I asked? The first cause is his collection of Russian paintings, which is very celebrated. When Mischa was arrested the KGB illegally confiscated all the paintings which were in his apartment. Rumor is that one of the paintings, a Kandinsky, went to Andropov's home (he was then head of the KGB, later premier). Three of Mischa's paintings are now in the Russian museum, and no one knows where the other pictures are. If Mischa is free he will demand his paintings. The pictures in her home which I see were also confiscated but she got them back through the courts. Mischa thinks all of this was organized against him because of the art collection. Also the KGB knows that Mischa knows a lot about the workings and history of the KGB. . . .

Hearing her for two hours describe this story, I thought many times how appropriate to use the abbreviation K. [Kafka] for her name. Again and again I felt the physical pressure to shake my head in disbelief. It was more than I could in some real sense accept as real, that it was not a novel, not a movie, it was this woman's son.

Mischa later, when he was freed, told me that the KGB had attempted to recruit him as a spy, reporting on the other physicists at his institute. When he not only refused, but in true Mischa style, threatened to expose their attempt, the KGB then accused him of being a CIA agent, and imprisoned him.

I visited Mischa's institute and found that a number of his colleagues were willing to be videotaped by me speaking out in his favor and against his being a CIA spy. A week later two of them, me, and Sasha Etkind were crowded into the tiny elevator on the way up to Mrs. K.'s apartment for the video session. When the elevator stalled and would not move for a few minutes, jokes were made that the KGB were on to us and had acted to prevent the videotaping. A joke, which I believe some of them, took seriously. After five minutes the elevator began to move; there were sighs of relief.

From my diary:

Tonight was a meeting at Mrs. K.'s home with a deputy from the Leningrad council, two members of the Institute committee formed to free Mischa, and two members of Memorial, an organization dedicated to those killed by Stalin. I videotaped more than two hours. It is fascinating and ghastly. A police state still continues; the KGB is as free as it ever was, and according to them, totally supported by Gorbachev. They were, according to Sasha Etkind, who translated, very radical people. They were inspiring by their outspoken bravery and courage and their demand for freedom and human rights. But it was terrible to hear new details about Mischa's imprisonment. For example, how he spent more than seven months on bread and water, manacled, in solitary. What an outrage! What contradictions this country is now—glasnost giving people the freedom to speak out without fear and criticize, but with the KGB in full force and the Party running and managing the government. I hope the videotapes I have made will be useful.

*Tomorrow I will leave it at the American consulate to be
sent through the diplomatic pouch.*

When I returned to America I sent the videotape and
my diary, from which I have been quoting, to Abe Rosenthal, who was then an editor and op-ed writer at the *New
York Times*. He had been outspoken about the plight of
political prisoners in the Soviet Union. Rosenthal wrote
a column about Mischa, and a few months later he was
freed. He and his mother both came immediately to San
Francisco. Mischa left her with us for a month while he
traveled to the few places left who wanted to hear about the
Gulag. It was no longer news, after more famous political
prisoners had been freed a few years earlier and gone on
speaking tours.

Mischa was the last and longest-held political prisoner
in Russia—fifteen years. Since his release he has lived in
the Boston area, very active in human rights. He helped
found the not-for-profit organization Freedom Channel,
supporting Russian groups active in building a civil society there. I have not heard from him or seen him since he
returned to my apartment to retrieve his mother and they
moved to Boston.

My second visit to Russia was under the auspices of a
UC exchange program with their government. Although
based in Leningrad, giving lectures at the university, I
was also sent first to Kiev and then to Moscow for a few
days each.

There was unrest in Kiev at the time of my visit, with
people in the streets waiving Ukrainian flags. Even then
they wanted independence from Russia. The Chernobyl

nuclear plant meltdown had occurred less than a month before. The people were told by the Soviets that there was nothing to fear from the radiation level in Kiev and the area surrounding Chernobyl. A pediatrician I met told me the children on his ward literally glowed from their overdose of radiation.

After my return to America, the CIA asked me if I would analyze a televised speech Gorbachev had given soon after the meltdown, reassuring the Ukrainian people that there was no need to evacuate, because the radiation level was not dangerous. Our government knew, from monitoring the radiation level, that it was very dangerous. We also believed that the Soviets had no means to evacuate a large number of people and no place to put them. Was Gorbachev lying, or had his people misinformed him about the danger, so he thought he was telling the truth? I regret now that I refused to make the judgment, would not even look at the video of his speech, because, I said, I had no data on how well I could detect lies by well-educated Soviets. I had proposed to do such a study so I would be prepared for such a request as the one they were making now, but the CIA had turned me down. I was not willing to go out on an untested limb.

CHAPTER 13

Catching Lies about Opinions and Taking Money

I CONTINUED TO SPEND nearly half my time precisely measuring how people behaved when they told different types of lies. In one experiment I repeated a scenario that had been used often in the polygraph literature, in which the subjects tell the truth or lie about whether they have taken the scientist's money, which is or is not on a table where they can be tempted. In another study, subjects had to tell the truth about a strongly held opinion or claim to believe the opposite of their true opinion. In both of these experiments the subjects were anyone who read an advertisement posted on telephone poles which said "You can earn $50 in 15 seconds', call this telephone number for an appointment." They would earn that much money if they succeeded in fooling the interrogator—me. I was highly motivated to catch them, as it was my personal money they would get if I didn't detect who was lying and who was truthful. I was very successful! Before each session began

I held up my book *Telling Lies*, told them that I wrote this book, I was an expert lie catcher. If they were telling the truth they had nothing to fear; I would know it. But if they were lying I would catch them. My purpose in this boast was to boost their apprehension detection if they were lying, which would then generate behavioral clues to deceit, and at the same time lower fear of being mistakenly judged by those who were being truthful.

There was also a threat of severe punishment, as severe as I could get the Institutional Review Board (IRB), the committee protecting human subjects, to approve. When each subject arrived at my lab to earn the $50, I explained that they would only get that much money if they got away with lying. If they told the truth, and were believed, they would only earn $10. But if they were accused of lying—like in the real world, it didn't matter whether they were actually lying or not, innocent people get jailed if the judge or jury convicts them—they would get punished.

I then gave them a taste of the punishment. They entered a totally dark room the size of a telephone booth, and once they were seated, they heard a sound as loud as a firecracker, just ten decibels below the level at which there is a risk of damaging hearing. When they came out of the room labeled in large letters "punishment chamber" I told them that if they were accused of lying they would have to be in the punishment chamber for sixty minutes and hear forty blasts of noise. If they didn't want to take that risk and opted not to participate in the experiment, I offered them $5 for their time so far. None refused. They were all males; no females responded to our posted invitations to participate.

We also ran a condition where the monetary rewards were the same, but with no punishment. Without the punishment our measurements failed to distinguish lying from truthfulness. The behaviors we had identified in the nursing study also occurred when people lied in the threat of punishment condition. When we showed one-minute samples from the taking money experiment and the opinion lie experiment, we again found that nearly everyone was at chance in making this judgment. Incidentally, those we trained with examples and the first version of what was to become the Micro Expressions Intensive Training Tool (METT Intensive) were accurate in spotting lies when they saw samples from the nurses, money, or opinion scenarios. And, those few who were accurate on the opinion samples were also accurate on the money and nurses samples. A lot of findings, all of which were published in various scientific journals over the decade from 1985 to 1995.

The finding that the behavioral clues to deceit are not lie-specific but occur regardless of the content of the lie when there was a threat of severe punishment is very relevant to answering the critics—such as the American Civil Liberties Union (ACLU)—of my efforts to train airport screening personnel to spot people with so-called "malintent." Findings from a huge field study conducted in multiple airports (which a congressional critic of the TSA [Transportation Security Administration] has been successful in blocking from publication) were very encouraging. Comparing the number of felons and smugglers caught when TSA personnel searched passengers who showed behavioral or other signs of malintent with the number caught when people were randomly selected,

TSA-trained people did fifty times better! The ACLU's complaint was that the TSA was not authorized to catch felons or smugglers, only terrorists.

TSA asked me to appear in a number of public forums to answer the ACLU. I was glad to do so. There are two answers. First, terrorism is a rare event, so it is no surprise a terrorist has not yet been caught in the U.S. trying to board an airplane. But we are catching what the police call "bad guys." Second, my research has shown that when the stakes are high and so is the threat of punishment, the same changes in behavior occur regardless of the specifics of what the lie is about. So, a lie to conceal a terrorist plan, a lie to conceal smuggling money, a lie to conceal being wanted for murder, a lie to conceal having an affair with an underage participant—all will generate the same changes in behavior. The bottom line: Behavioral clues to deceit are not unique to what the lie is about.

Soon after *Telling Lies* was published, a training officer from the Bureau of Alcohol, Tobacco, and Firearms (ATF) who had read my book visited my lab, asking me if I would offer training to members of ATF. Before showing him any of the training, I asked him to take one of the lie-catching tests. He scored 90 percent or 100 percent on each test I gave him, the nurses, the money, and the opinion tests. I called him a "wizard of deception detection," and searched through my data for any other wizards. And indeed, there were a few. This discovery launched the Wizards project, which Maureen O'Sullivan helped me pursue. After a year during which we each interviewed wizards we had identified she asked if she could take it over completely. I agreed. Unfortunately, when she died unexpectedly a few years later all the data she had collected (she had interviewed more than 30 wizards) was lost. All that remains is the early finding that many of the wizards had dealt successfully with a trauma early in their life.

CHAPTER 14

Television and Violence, 1970

MY FIRST FORAY into the world of television happened in 1970. As a result, I did get an important new finding about facial expressions: the expressions shown when witnessing violence on TV predicted whether a boy would afterward help or try to harm another boy. Our measurements of girls' facial expressions, which were similar to those shown by the boys, didn't predict whether girls would subsequently help or hurt. I never could find out why.

In 1970, Senator John Pastore wanted an answer to the question of whether watching violence on TV generates an increase in violent behavior. In response, under the auspices of the surgeon general with guidance from NIMH, a million dollars was allotted to get an answer in one year. I was approached by NIMH, wrote a brief proposal, and was given $100,000, which, corrected for inflation would be $600,000 today—a lot of money. I recruited parents to bring their young children into my lab. While some of the children waited ostensibly for the experiment to begin, we showed a five-minute excerpt from the *Untouchables* program in which there were three killings and a view of a victim's suffering. As a comparison group, other children instead saw an excerpt from a footrace while they were in the waiting room, which had as much activity and competition, but no violence. After viewing the TV programs the children each came into an adjacent room to play a game.

The game had been invented by Leonard Berkowitz at the University of Wisconsin.[35] The child was shown a wheel, which when turned produced a piece of candy for each revolution. The child was told that there was another child next door, who would be turning another wheel. If the child who had seen the TV programs pressed the green "help" button, the wheel of the child next door would turn faster producing more candy for that child. If the child pressed the red "hurt" button, the handle on the wheel would get so hot that it would hurt the other child when that child tried to turn the wheel.

Everyone hated my results. Parents groups did not like that I had found that watching TV violence made some children more helpful. Those were the kids who had shown sadness and pain on their face when they saw the TV clip. The television industry attacked me because I had shown that watching TV made some children try to hurt other children. Those were the kids who had shown glee on their face when they watched the violence. And Ralph Nader attacked me.

Nader asked if there was really another child in the other room. Since there wasn't, in his eyes I had unethically lied to the children, leading them to think there was. I asked if he would have approved of my having another child in the other room, who could be hurt or helped. No, he would not. I asked if he thought it was important to find out whether TV violence encouraged at least some children to hurt others. Yes, but not this way. How? He didn't know.

My experiment was the first I know of to show that the specific emotions shown in facial expression predicts how people will act subsequently, at least for boys. I published my findings in a report to the surgeon general. That choice was as good as burying it. Since publication, it has been cited rarely. A mistake on my part, but I was getting tired of the bureaucracy and disputes I always encountered when I tried to publish in a reputable scientific journal. With more than one hundred submissions to journals, the overwhelming majority were rejected initially. It usually took a year or two of fighting to get a paper published, the whole process occupying about two years, and it was very aggravating. My perseverance to overcome initial rejection is an instance of the first of the four mottos that have guided my life: Never take no for an answer.

The other three mottos are: Leave no stone unturned, Aim higher than you can see, and Never give up hope. When I left home at fifteen, full of guilt and completely lacking any confidence in myself, I would repeat these mottos to myself again and again. I don't remember where I got them, but I still resurrect them when I encounter some obstacle or opportunity.

The TV network executives dismissed my findings as meaningless because I was only studying a child's reactions to a few minutes of TV, in children who had likely already seen hundreds if not thousands of hours of TV. That got me mad. I decided to find a way to examine the effect of twenty hours of TV, a big jump from the five minutes in my experiment that they were criticizing, on children who had never seen TV. I got a grant from the National Science Foundation and another from the Markle Foundation to pursue this goal.

I collaborated with Robert Liebert, a professor of psychology at State University of New York at Stony Brook, and we developed two TV "diets." Each provided two hours a day for two weeks of either violent or prosocial TV (which showed collaboration and cooperation, not violence, competition, and exploitation). I developed a scoring system to measure how kids behaved during the free play sessions in the school playground. Would those who were fed a TV diet of violence bully other kids or show other antisocial behaviors? South Africa was the last industrialized country that, for political reasons, did not yet have TV. I went to South Africa, explained the study plan, and recruited professors of psychology at four universities in four South African cities to run the project. They did, with thousands of children. Unexpectedly, the South African government seized the data before it could be analyzed, never explaining why. That was the end of that project.

I didn't give up; it is not my style. I should have, but I thought I could still get some interesting findings by going to Micronesia. A friend, who was working on related issues with the Micronesian Congress, told me that the Micronesian politicians were worried that when TV was introduced it might harm the different cultures in the different islands in Micronesia.

I flew out, visiting two different cultures. In Ponape, there was very little violence and relaxed child rearing. The members of this culture were scattered across many small islands. All the adolescents came in to each district's center, living there for four years to attend the one high school for that district. During the four years the kids were in the district center they were the responsibility of the head of the district center. I convinced him of the value of the study, and he agreed I could conduct it there, providing consent to participate for the high schoolers.

I also visited Truk, a culture known for its aggressiveness and a high incidence of violent acts. It was the same routine: the kids from the scattered islands making up this culture all came in to live at the district center to attend high school, giving oversight to the head of the district center. He also gave consent for the kids to participate in our study.

Micronesia offered the opportunity to find out the impact of TV violence in both an aggressive and also a peaceful culture, in which no TV had yet been seen! I had all the materials: the two "diets" of TV programs and the routines on how to measure aggression in the playgrounds. All I needed was clearance from the UCSF IRB, the committee that reviews research to ensure the protection of human subjects. That committee knew me, for they had earlier approved my studies in which I showed gory films to student nurses and used a hidden camera to record their behavior.

Incidentally, after that nurses experiment I revealed the hidden cameras to the nursing students, explaining I had done that so they wouldn't be self-conscious. At that point no one had seen the video we had recorded, as I did not use a cameraman. I gave them a number of choices: have me erase the videos; let me use the video in my research; allow other scientists to examine the video records; show excerpts in classrooms for teaching; and allow excerpts to be shown on TV. No one asked me to erase the videos. Some of them restricted the use, while other student nurses agreed and were shown on the TV program *20/20* when there was a twelve-minute segment about my work.

I applied to the committee on human research for clearance, explaining the procedures and that they had been approved not only by the district heads, but also by the Micronesian Congress. They turned me down. They wanted the parents to consent. I applied again explaining that the parents did not know what TV is and I could not get to them, for they were scattered in islands across a portion of the ocean as large as the United States. Each application took about a week to prepare and then it would be four to six weeks before I would learn the outcome. By this point I had lost four months trying to get approval.

I was turned down once again. If I couldn't get the approval of the parents, they wanted letters from the district heads approving my procedure. I wrote to the district heads, and it took about six months for me to get a letter to them and a response to come back. They both replied that they did not know this committee, they knew me, and had agreed to work with me. They refused to write to this unknown committee. I reported their refusal to the human subjects committee, and a month later, they switched to wanting a letter from the Micronesian

Congress. By now, I had lost ten or eleven months trying to get approval. I wrote to the person responsible in the Micronesian Congress who had endorsed the project, losing nearly six months for him to get my letter and for me to get his response. Like the district heads, he refused to write to people he did not know. By now I had lost almost eighteen months.

After another month of waiting, the human subjects committee finally gave their approval. But before I could get out to Micronesia, commercial television came in. I had spent more than two years, initially going out to Micronesia and then trying to overcome the obstacles set by my colleagues on the human subjects committee. Although they never acknowledged this, my hunch is that they didn't like me "polluting" these innocent cultures with TV, ignoring that these cultures wanted me to find out before, inevitably, commercial TV came. Soon after commercial TV was shown, rapes and a burglary occurred, which had never happened before.

The university bureaucracy had blocked me. I had lost nearly three years. Ralph Nader had attacked me. The government of South Africa had destroyed my project there. The university committee had through their delays killed the opportunity in Micronesia. I gave up—no more research on TV violence.

.

My mother and father, 1942.

Six-year-old Paul in Atlantic City, 1940.

First Lieutenant Paul Ekman, Army Psychologist.

Silvan Tomkins, who had a major influence in my thinking about the face.

Swedish psychologist Carl-Herman Hjortsjö, creator of the mimic language later to be used in my Facial Action Coding System (FACS).

Friend and colleague, Wally Friesen.

Waseda University with Professor Tomita (left) during our cross-cultural study of Japanese and American display rules, 1969.

In Russia as a Fulbright lecturer at Leningrad State University with my official host, Marc Lasko (far right), 1979.

Mary Ann and I on our wedding day, 1979.

With Ron Simons, friend and collaborator on *Startle Responses*, 1979.

Me in my 30s.

CHAPTER 15

Creating a Young Generation of Emotion Scientists

STAN SCHNEIDER, an official in the research fellow-ship branch of NIMH, whom I got to know when I held a pre-doctoral, then a postdoctoral, fellowship and later received a Career Scientist Award from that branch of NIMH, approached me with an idea I then ran with. (Note that once again, the idea was not mine—it wasn't my idea to identify deception clues or do the cross-cultural research—but I recognized the merits of the ideas and pounced on them, making them happen.)

Stan's idea was to generate a young generation of emotion researchers by creating a postdoctoral training program in emotion. He recognized it could become a very active research area, but there was no university at that time that had the talent to train young psychologists to become faculty specializing in emotion. A postdoctoral training program could fill the gap.

Stan later wrote about the program in 1995 after it had been running for a number of years. He said the seed for his interest in developing the field of emotion was planted after a meeting of the Eastern Psychological Association in 1976. He had dinner one night with Silvan Tomkins and Rae Carlson (a personality researcher who was to become Silvan's lover). "It was a memorable evening. I was dining with stellar representatives of areas of real weakness in NIMH's training portfolio, and the evening . . . ended for me with the conviction that emotion research warranted a higher profile in the NIMH training program."

Stan knew it would take a consortium linking various universities to provide the needed training. Stan wrote, "the . . . indispensable part of an emotion consortium was The Person . . . who could provide the necessary leadership, who had the energy, the vision, the knowledge, the patience, and the contacts to make this work. . . . I suggested the matter of an emotion consortium to Paul Ekman. . . . He surely had the necessary vision to lead the program. Paul's energy and his ability to stimulate interest and to whet the appetites of emotion researchers were major ingredients in the success of getting the venture underway."

These quotes from what Stan wrote I have just now read for the first time. I didn't know that Silvan had planted the seed, nor did I know that Stan back in the mid 1980s had such regard for me.

I contacted scientists at fourteen universities who were studying emotion, asking them to join the consortium. Each of them would spend a week in San Francisco, where I expected to house the program at UCSF, giving a formal talk to an emotion seminar I planned to lead. They would then meet individually with each of the postdoctoral fellows. They would also be expected to spend two weeks in San Francisco every summer, participating with the other faculty from the Bay Area and around the country in a workshop on emotion. And, they would be eligible to have a postdoctoral fellow assigned to them for two years, at their university. They would be listed on the announcement of the program, but it would be up to the applicants as to whom they chose to work with. I did stipulate that they would have to agree to the requirement that a fellow who came to their lab for two years would be able to generate at least one research article on which they were first or solo author. A few potential faculty members refused to participate because of that requirement. Out of the fourteen potential faculty members I attempted to recruit, eleven agreed.

My plan was to have a three-year fellowship during which the first year would be spent in a laboratory in the S.F. Bay Area (encompassing emotion labs at Stanford, UC Berkeley, and UC Davis, in addition to my lab). Participants would also attend a weekly all-day seminar. Two weeks were devoted to the visits of each of the eleven members of the consortium. In the first of those two weeks, the participants would spend the day formulating questions after having read articles assigned by the consortium faculty member under scrutiny. The following week the consortium faculty member would begin the day by addressing the questions that had been sent to him or her. The discussion was intense and lasted all day. The rest of the week was spent in individual meetings with each of the postdoctoral fellows.

After the completion of the first year, the next two years would be spent at another lab, with a different member of the consortium. By the end of the fellowships, each of the fellows would have experience in two different research methods and, through the seminar and the summer workshops, would learn about diverse approaches to emotion. We would select six fellows in year one, and six more in the fourth year of the program. I also allowed some of the graduate students at Berkeley to attend the weekly seminar and the summer workshops. Many of them went on to have very successful research careers.

Stan liked my plan but suggested that I also recruit Richard Lazarus to co-lead the weekly seminar. Ten years older than me, Lazarus was an established researcher with a connection to a psychology department (at Berkeley), so the program would not be only sponsored by a psychiatry department faculty member—me. I did so. Lazarus, who did little other than show up at the seminar and workshops, was congenial. [I later learned that he used his participation in the seminar to get halftime release from teaching.]

I had first met Dick Lazarus when I was twenty, an undergraduate applying to the Ph.D. program at Clark University, where he, at age thirty, was an assistant professor faculty member. He interviewed me. A ten-year difference was an enormous gap at that point in life. By the time the postdoctoral training program began, the age difference still played a role, but much less. We were both professors, we were both well-known scientists, he more than me, but the difference in our repute was not great. We became close friends.

He was generous in providing me both with the emotion-arousing films he had used in his own research, which I used in my display rule study. He also introduced me to the faculty member who he had worked with at Waseda University. In the last twenty years of his life, between his sixties and early eighties, I was still trailing him by ten years, but that age gap became increasingly irrelevant. Near the end of his life Dick told me he was worried that when he died the obituary that would appear about him in the main journal, the *American Psychologist*, would not do him justice. I suggested that he write his own obit ahead of time, give it to me, and when he died I would write the *American Psychologist*, volunteering to write his obit, using what he wrote. That is what happened.

In 1989, I learned that the program was funded. It was the largest training program the NIMH had ever funded. The applicants were numerous and outstanding. They were knowledgeable about the nature of the program, and in their application they specified the faculty member they wished to work with in year one and the second faculty member they wished to work with in years two and three of the program. We selected the best applicants, with the proviso that no faculty member could get more than one postdoctoral fellow in the first round.

When I announced the good news that the program had been funded, I asked the chairman of psychiatry for one large room for the seminar and for the six post-doctoral fellows. The chairman turned me down saying "emotion is not relevant to psychiatry." He was still mad at me over a disagreement a few years earlier regarding whether an assistant professor should be promoted to a tenured position. I agreed with the chairman's evaluation of the merits of the fellow up for such a promotion, and would have agreed he should be turned down but I learned that an important procedural mistake had been made depriving him of warning that he was not on track to be promoted. That should have occurred in a pre-tenure review three years ahead of when the final decision would be made. It had not occurred. I insisted that even though the normal six years were now up, he had to be given the pre-tenure review and three more years. Infuriated, the chairman tried unsuccessfully to lower my salary and take away my secretarial support. After I blocked these punishments, he now had the authority to block my pursuit of this postdoctoral training program by not giving me any space.

I moved the training program to Berkeley where they were delighted to have it, and that is where it stayed during the six years I directed the program. My colleague and friend Robert Levenson helped me with the seminar after Lazarus passed away, and looked after the local administrative issues.

The psychiatry department chairman at UCSF, who had rejected the program, did not have his own chairmanship renewed. The head of the committee that reviewed his first five years as chairman and would decide whether his position should be renewed told me that one of the main reasons they would recommend against renewal of his chairmanship was his rejection of this training program, which could have brought stellar faculty from around the country, even one from Europe, to our university. I have to admit that I was very pleased.

The training program was very successful, the applicants were superb, and more than half of them were to later become faculty at major universities. By the sixth year, the quality of the applicants lessened, which I attributed to the shortage of positions available at major research-oriented universities. It no longer made sense to take a three-year fellowship if you could get one of the increasingly scarce faculty positions. Because of that and noting the shrinking of the professoriate I decided to withdraw from the program. Richie Davidson, a member of the postdoctoral training program faculty from the start, a good friend, and sometime research collaborator, offered to take it over and run it from Madison at the University of Wisconsin, which he did.

CHAPTER 16

Saint Busting

A CLINICAL PSYCHOLOGIST named Jeannine Herron recruited me to join a team organized at the request of Father Laurentin, the Vatican's investigator (and debunker) of reports of miraculous experiences. She was the POC (the point of contact) between us and the Vatican. Jeannine, her husband, and young children spent a year sailing around the world, and she wrote a book about it. That got a lot of credit and admiration from me.

As an expert on lying, I was asked to evaluate a middle-aged woman from Los Angeles who claimed to be having discussions with the Holy Mother in a daily forty-minute trance at the same time every afternoon. She claimed to be receiving messages from the Holy Mother about what Jesus wanted. For some time the messages were about bringing an end to one or another sin, but more recently Jesus reportedly wanted a church built at a specific location in the Los Angeles area. The woman had achieved a large following that was prepared to raise the needed funds. The local parish priest, whom the visionary reported to daily on her experiences, had been in touch with the Vatican; hence the team was formed to evaluate her.

I enlisted my colleague Bob Levenson to examine her physiology during the trances, and a neurologist John Mueller at the local VA hospital to join with me. I first interviewed her for an hour, after being briefed by Father Laurentin, who asked me to look for signs of lying and signs of the devil! I translated the second part of his request to how the devil might feel, expecting to see expressions of enjoyable anger or enjoyable contempt. She had Turner syndrome, a chromosomal abnormality that affects appearance and prevents pregnancy, but had no known cognitive impairment.

I found her to be a concerned, sincere woman who showed neither signs of lying, nor the aforementioned signs of the devil. I asked her if she would be willing to come to our laboratory, so we could observe her during a trance. She agreed, we did, and the results were amazing!

We video-recorded her. Her eyes were open for forty minutes, but she never blinked! I did not know it was possible to prevent blinks for even five minutes, let alone forty. My neurologist friend put a wisp of cotton repeatedly in her eye, yet she failed to show the reflexive response to that intrusion. While Levenson monitored her heart rate, blood pressure, skin conductance, and temperature, we repeatedly tried to startle her with a blast of very loud white noise. She had no visible response and no changes in the physiology that we measured. She clearly was in an altered state, but what was happening within that state there was no way to know.

Father Laurentin did not seem disappointed in my report. At least he could rule out lying and had evidence that her trances were real events. He asked me if I would join him in evaluating other claims for exceptional powers that he had to evaluate. He could keep me busy full time, he said. I declined.

A neuropsychologist on the faculty at UC Medical School also examined her. He reported to us that she had extraordinary powers. He would put his hands behind his back in fists, from which he would show different numbers of fingers. Although he was certain she could not see what he was doing, she never failed to guess correctly how many fingers he was releasing. I didn't know whether to believe him.

Thinking about it now, I am not as surprised by what we found as I was then. I had no way to account for what we found, let alone what my colleague claimed. I have learned in recent years that though there are a number of matters I can't explain, that does not mean they don't exist. Only that they are not understandable by contemporary scientific thinking. I discuss this matter further when I describe the impact the Dalai Lama had on me.

CHAPTER 17

Turning on the Physiology of Emotion, 1983–1990

BY ACCIDENT, once again, I made an important discovery that made the front page of the *New York Times*. It was not planned, but a complete surprise.

When Wally Friesen and I were making the various expressions necessary to develop the Facial Action Coding System (FACS), which I described earlier, we sometimes had very strong physical sensations. After about six months, one of us brought this up to the other. Once we knew it was happening to both of us, we focused on which voluntary facial actions were generating the sensations in our body. Incidentally, those sensations were quite unpleasant to experience.

It was only when we made one of the combinations of facial muscular actions that generated one of the facial expressions we had found to be universal that we felt these very strong physical sensations. Facial expressions were not simply a display system. They also could generate emotion, at least the sensations felt during emotional experience. The arrows went both ways! Digging through Stanislavsky's writings I found that he had not only talked about how memories generate emotion, but also said "make the movement and the feeling would follow"!

I wrote a grant to acquire the equipment necessary to measure changes in Autonomic Nervous System (ANS) activity, but was turned down on the grounds that I didn't have a track record doing this kind of research. They were right, so we put it aside. A few years later, John Gottman, one of my most esteemed scientific colleagues, who had been using a FACS-based scoring system to study dysfunctional marriages, wrote to me suggesting that I accept Bob Levenson as a yearlong sabbatical visitor. Bob was then an associate professor at Indiana University and just what we needed, an expert on the ANS (the Autonomic Nervous System, as distinguished from the CNS, the Central Nervous System). I wrote John that I never take a postdoctoral or pre-doctoral visitor without first meeting them and ensuring it will be congenial. We were at that point a small lab, only about fifteen people. John assured me that I would like Bob, and that I should trust his judgment. He was right; Bob became a close friend as well as a great collaborator over the next decades.

Bob was on the verge of quitting psychology and returning to his love of music, at which he had considerable talent playing the saxophone. I take some credit for bringing him back into psychology, reigniting the excitement of groundbreaking research. He now combines two careers: psychology and leading two bands, in which he also plays. Amazingly, he does both extremely well and is now recognized internationally as *the* expert on the psychophysiology of emotion. The kind of research I do now is unrelated to his specialty, but I often seek his advice about problems I encounter in research or in getting what I find published—a never-ending problem and source of misery—and on the abundance of health problems that have plagued my last decade.

Soon after Bob arrived, he remembers being told that I would not talk to him until he learned FACS. I don't remember making such a demand; it is a bit embarrassing! What I remember is telling him about our discovery that making the right expression turned on the physiology of emotion, which he thought was sufficiently off-beat and contradictory to the main ideas in cognitive psychology about emotion—that emotions can only be generated by an appraisal/cognitive process—to interest him.

We borrowed some equipment from a colleague and ran the experiment, in which I coached the participants in how to make each of the universal facial expressions. This task we later named the DFA, the Directed Facial Action procedure. No one had trouble making all of the facial movements for surprise and disgust, and most of the facial movements involved in fear, anger, and sadness. But enjoyment was a problem if we required that the expression involve not just smiling lips, but contraction of the outer muscle that orbits the eye, AU 6 in FACS terminology, *orbicularis oculi, pars lateralis* in anatomical terms. Only about 20 percent of our subjects could make this movement, a finding we verified in later research identifying the facial movements that are hard or easy to make voluntarily.

We found strong differences in ANS activity for fear, anger, sadness, and disgust, but little differentiation for smiling. This finding was so unexpected in the traditional view of emotion, which had specified that emotions occur only after an appraisal of some event, or a memory, that we got it published in the most prestigious journal, *Science*, in 1983. We also made the front page of the *New York Times*, although they got the story completely wrong! Dan Goleman, who was to become a close friend, later told me that he was just in the process of being considered as a new science writer for the *Times*. When asked about the importance of our publication, which had just appeared in *Science*, Dan said it was very important.

Howard Shenck was then the *Times*'s only science writer, and his story, accompanied by a cartoon-like illustration, claimed just what we had *not* found: smile and you turn on the physiology of enjoyment. A good story, but it was anger, fear, disgust, and sadness that had distinctive patterns of ANS physiology, not smiling! A decade later in a series of studies collaboratively with Richie (Richard J.) Davidson (University of Wisconsin) we found that what I called the Duchenne smile (in FACS terms both the smiling muscle AU 12 and the outer portion of the muscle that orbits the eye, AU 6) generated the central nervous system (CNS) activity associated with enjoyment (as measured by EEG). More about that later.

To this day cognitive psychologists who focus on emotion dismiss our findings if they don't ignore them completely. It is not my fault, I have claimed, that nature provided multiple ways to access emotion. The cognitive psychologists who reviewed my grant proposal to analyze, for the first time, multiple ways of accessing different emotions (memory, watching film clips, and the DFA) with multiple measures (FACS scoring of the face, ANS physiology, and self-report) caused it to be rejected. One of them explained to me that, despite the many supporting experiments Levenson and I had by then published, he would not believe my findings because it didn't fit his theory! It took me five years without funds to analyze the results, and out of combination of spite and wanting to move on to other research I have never published the findings.

There were two very important findings; I report them here for the first time in print.

First, it doesn't matter how you accessed the emotion— films, remembering, or the DFA—the facial expressions and ANS physiology were the same. Put more generally: there are multiple paths for turning on an emotion, but once activated the emotional activity is the same regardless of the path that activated it. Later, this finding was to become very important in replying to the critics of the TSA's SPOT (Screening Passengers with Observational Techniques), which I helped create.

Second, the changes in different aspects of emotional activity are coherent, inter-correlated. A change in ANS was related to a change in facial activity. This supports an idea put forth by Silvan Tomkins two decades earlier— that emotional activity is run by a central set of instructions, different for each emotion, which he called the *affect program*.

For the next decade, Levenson and I did a series of experiments, closing off possible loopholes that might have undermined our findings. We even did a cross-cultural replication to establish that this was not culture specific, but instead a universal phenomenon. I turned to my friend

Karl Heider, the anthropologist whom I described in Chapter 6, who had set out to prove my findings wrong about the universality of some facial expressions and instead replicated what I had found in his work in another remote area of Papua New Guinea

Heider was then living, with his family, in the highlands of Sumatra, in the town of Bukittinggi, among the Minangkabau. Although not visually isolated, as were the people I had studied and the people Karl had studied in different spots in Papua New Guinea, these people were as different from Western cultures as could be found in the mid-1980s. They were not only extreme in their Islamic views, but also matrilineal, with inheritance through the mother's, not the father's, side of the family, the husband going to live with his wife's family. One manifestation of this combination of beliefs was that a woman was bossed by her brother, not her husband.

Levenson wears his hair long, in a Louis the 14th style. I was warned by Heider that the immigration officials in Sumatra would not allow someone with such long hair to enter their country. I convinced Bob to trim his hair; a noble sacrifice for science. When we arrived in Panang, the entry spot for Sumatra, we had more than a dozen suitcases loaded with equipment. Heider advised us not to report the equipment as it would be either taxed or confiscated. As we gathered all the suitcases at the airport, Heider and his children were on the other side of the barrier, but could easily see us. One of Heider's sons recognized me, and ran across the barrier to hug me. That distracted the custom officials, who then waved us through. Indonesians are very family friendly.

It took a week to set up the laboratory to measure the ANS physiology and facial expressions. We then conducted a series of experiments, working very long days, using the DFA (the directed facial action task) as well as some experiments judging facial expressions. For the first time I was able to test the recognition of contempt, which I had, for reasons I no longer remember, left out of the research in New Guinea. Contempt recognition, differentiated from disgust and all the other emotions, was extremely good. And we found, as expected, the same ANS physiology results when the Sumatrans made the different facial expressions called for in the DFA. No surprise to us, it was what we expected to find, but we had to test it to be certain and publish our findings.

NUMBER 6 *Voluntarily made facial expressions can generate the physiology of emotion.*

There are four side stories to this adventure in Bukittinggi:

I discovered the most painful spot on your body to apply the output from a cold-water shower—the armpits.

Levenson and I ate the same food every day, morning, noon, and night except one night at a restaurant he ordered something called "deng-deng," which I would not even taste. Over time he became very sick, and when we returned to San Francisco the tropical disease specialists couldn't diagnose or treat him. When it got so bad that he couldn't get out of bed, I arranged for him to go to the Mayo Clinic. He recovered, but is dependent on medications that he takes to this day, enabling him to lead a very active, full life.

The third side story was a phone call from Shelly Korchin, then head of the clinical psychology program at Berkeley. Shelly was a friend of Silvan Tomkins, who looked me up when he came to Berkeley. We sometimes went fishing together. Shelly told me they were considering Bob for a tenured full professorship. He asked me if my sister was depressed would I send her to Bob for treatment. I said I would not, as Bob's expertise is not as a psychotherapist. But I would send her to Bob if she wanted to study physiological changes in depression. They hired him.

The last story is still upsetting to me now more than twenty-five years later, as it led to the bitter ending of my until then very close relationship with Silvan Tomkins. While still in Bukittinggi I received a long, angry letter from Silvan, in which he claimed I was stealing credit from him. The *Smithsonian* magazine had run a cover story (with pictures of me making faces on the cover) on facial expression. When they interviewed me I had told them they must talk to Silvan as he played an important role in my research, that he was the pioneer, not me. When they called me just before publication for a final "fact-check" I asked them to read me also what they had written about Silvan. They had forgotten to interview him, and they could now only add one sentence at most. I asked that they say there had been two influences on my thinking, Tomkins and Darwin. Silvan later complained: "Did you have to mention Darwin?"

In correspondence I told him that I was not the author of the article, and I attempted to be certain they included him. We arranged by mail for me to visit him at his oceanside home on the New Jersey shore when I returned.

I brought with me photocopies of all the places I had credited him in my publications since we met. I reminded him that before I published anything I always sent it to him for his approval that I had properly cited him. I also reminded him that since we met he had not published anything, while I had published many articles in major journals and a number of books. The only reason he was still remembered was because I kept citing him. Silvan said he loved me, but I was like his sister, a long-standing rival. I told him he had it wrong; I was not his sibling but his intellectual son.

A year later, I heard from Shelly Korchin that Silvan had visited him in Berkeley. I was deeply offended. I wrote to Silvan that the only other person who had visited the Bay Area without calling me was my father, and I would not tolerate being treated this way again from someone I had long loved. I told him I wanted to never see or hear from him again. And, I did not. Silvan died six years later at the age of 80. Wikipedia's entry on him includes a number of pictures of me, none with Silvan, and many of the photographs I took in New Guinea. No mention of the story told here of the denouement of our once very close relationship, told here for the first time in print.

CHAPTER 18

What Is an Emotion?

BY GOOD FORTUNE, not my doing, I met Ron Simons and subsequently did a study with him, which focused my attention on what distinguishes a reflex from an emotion. When I met him, Ron was a psychiatrist at Michigan State who did sophisticated cross-cultural research. He was such a serious scholar and researcher that he took the very relevant but highly unusual step of spending his sabbatical year as a postdoctoral fellow in anthropology at UC Berkeley in 1974, the same year his first ethnographic film on a Hindu festival was published.[36] He heard me give a lecture and wrote to me asking for an appointment, which was the seed for an important collaboration and an enduring close friendship.

Soon after his sabbatical he began to study Latah, which is the name given in Malaysia to those people who are easily startled. When that happens, their reactions are intense, often involving imitations of the actions of those around them. Latah is recognized also among the Ainu of Japan. Ron speculated that Latah exists pan-culturally although it is acknowledged in only a few cultures.

He was right. When he advertised in the East Lansing newspaper for people who had problems being easily startled, sure enough people contacted him, and their histories fit what had been described for Latah! We agreed to do a joint study of normal people and what we called "hyper-startlers" finding a larger reaction among the hyper-startlers, and unlike most people, no reduction in the magnitude of the startle if they were notified exactly when a loud noise would occur.

Our joint paper reported these findings, but most importantly it began to describe what distinguishes emotions from other mental states. It may not be obvious on first thought, but defining emotion is a tricky matter, for it is not just emotions that have distinctive feelings—pain, hunger, exhaustion also have distinctive feelings but aren't emotions. Seven years later, with more data on what emotions are, and using what I had learned in distinguishing a reflex from an emotion, I described nine characteristics that distinguish emotions from other mental states. But I forgot those I had written about in the paper with Ron, to which I now add, for the first time, four more characteristics to the list:

1. Distinctive universal signal (face and/or voice)

2. Presence in other primates (emotions are not unique to humans)

3. Distinctive physiology creates and sustains each emotion

4. Distinctive universals in some of the antecedent events that trigger each emotion

5. Quick onset

6. Brief duration

7. Automatic appraisal, which occurs out of conscious awareness

8. Unbidden occurrence

Here are the four to be added to the list from the 1985 paper with Ron:

9. Very few triggers that will always call forth the same emotion in all people; a qualification of characteristic #4

10. The signal can be suppressed

11. The signal can be simulated well enough to mislead most people

12. It can be enacted in either a constructive or destructive way; constructiveness being based on whether the way in which the emotion is enacted furthers or interferes with further collaboration with the other(s) involved in the emotional event. (This characteristic grew out of my series of discussions with the Dalai Lama from 2003 to 2012, described later.)

CHAPTER 19

A Fight with the Dean and Chancellor

MY LAB ALMOST CLOSED for the third time in the early 1990s when the dean of the medical school and the chancellor of UCSF sought revenge for my having opposed them when they attempted to terminate the chairman of the psychiatry department, Robert Wallerstein. (I earlier described the two near catastrophes when my lab nearly closed: in 1965 when the site visitors from NIMH recommended disapproval of my request to renew my first grant [page 46], and when I nearly ran out of funds in 1976.) It is going to take quite a few pages to explain, and I was initially uncertain whether it was worth writing about. But it is part of the backstory about what a scientist, well recognized by his own university's scientists and whose work was becoming known to the public, had to deal with in order to survive. The two people who ran the university nearly drowned me. So here it is, without mentioning their names, only their titles.

First let me explain who Robert Wallerstein was, why the dean wanted to get rid of him, why I opposed that, and how then a few years later the dean sought his revenge. Wallerstein was a senior figure in psychoanalysis, not a personal friend, but impressive as a chairman. I had always followed the practice of sending whomever was chairman a copy of every article or book that I published. No chairman had ever responded before Wallerstein, who read and sent me comments on what I sent him. He also chaired grand rounds, the weekly departmental conference, asked the first question, and implied that everyone should attend this intellectual gathering of the department. Most of the faculty, for the first time, participated in the grand rounds.

I did not find Freudian theory, which Wallerstein endorsed, to be of much use in my research. In later years I was to comment on how Freud had ignored emotion, and as a result most contemporary psychoanalysts were completely unaware of the new research on emotion. But I thought Wallerstein was a serious and scholarly person, and was surprised when the outcome of the review of his chairmanship was to terminate his chairmanship. Such reviews are mandated every five years, but rarely in a medical school is anyone terminated; it is usually a lifetime post, unless the chair wishes to resign.

The review committee had not interviewed me, although I was a full professor, and was the only member of the department to have received the highest honor the academic senate awards for research accomplishments (in 1982). (It took another thirty years before another member of the psychiatry department was so honored by the academic senate.) I called a few other full professors of psychology; none of them had been interviewed by the review committee, despite the fact that the department had become, under Wallerstein's chairmanship, nearly equally split between medical and non-medical faculty. I was to learn later that was one of the reasons the dean and chancellor wanted to get rid of him!

Before I knew this, with naïve faith in the fairness of the review process, I wrote a letter to the dean, with a copy to Wallerstein, saying that the review of his chairmanship was invalid because half of the department's senior faculty, all those who were professors of psychology, had not been interviewed by the review committee. The dean asked me to meet with him.

The dean said he respected me, noting my publications in *Science* (the most prestigious scientific journal). Surely, he said, I could understand why they could not retain someone who appointed so many psychologists. I was shocked that he would say that to me. He went on to criticize Wallerstein for having recently appointed biological psychiatrists and psychologists who were out of the mainstream of current work on the neuroscientific basis of mental disorders. I agreed with the dean about the poor appointments, but I explained that Wallerstein had trusted the head of research within the department, a biological psychiatrist, to make the appointments. He should have known himself who should be appointed, the dean said. Wallerstein was out of touch with current work in biological psychiatry. I could not disagree with that.

Wallerstein filed a lawsuit against the University for Wrongful Termination of his chairmanship, citing my letter, which had documented that the review of his performance had been defective. I organized a petition of support, first getting those I knew did support him, and then asking his opponents, all but one of whom signed the petition rather than publicly acknowledge their opposition. Wallerstein asked me to negotiate with the dean's representative, which I did, earning him two more years as chairman and clerical support indefinitely once he returned to the status of a faculty member within the department.

I didn't realize until a few years later how much resentment I had earned. Let me explain the crisis that developed that gave the dean and the chancellor the opportunity to punish me. The MacArthur Foundation had given me a large grant, nearly a million dollars in the early 1990s, with the specification that I could bank the money and add to the grant the interest that accrued. I did so for three years, spending down my government grants, while the MacArthur funds grew. After three years MacArthur wrote that I had to return the grant funds, including the interest, because I had failed to provide the required yearly reports. The head of the university's financial management section that had received the money from MacArthur wrote to them, saying it was their fault, not mine. They had lost MacArthur's instructions during a move of their facilities, and had never told me that a yearly report was required. MacArthur wrote back that they didn't care who was at fault, their grant funds had to be returned!

The dean of the medical school announced that he was going to return the funds, leaving my laboratory without any funding. The chancellor refused to see me, and when the dean met with me, he told me that my lab would close but it would only take me a few years to get the government funds to open again. I explained that I would have to interrupt projects halfway completed and fire people who had been working with me for fifteen years. That's your bad luck, he said. I protested that this was occurring because the university had not met its fiduciary responsibility for managing the MacArthur grant, which their administrator had acknowledged. It did not matter, he said with a grin, he was going to return the funds and leave me penniless.

Unknown to the dean, the university's attorney contacted me, saying he believed the university was acting unethically if not illegally, suggesting I stop them with an injunction. I hired the best-known attorney in San Francisco, and got that injunction preventing the dean from returning the grant funds to MacArthur. A few days later a senior official at NIMH who had been involved in the many years of grant support I had received called. He reported that the dean had called him, complaining about me, questioning why they had supported me all these years. I asked the NIMH official if he would be willing to testify about the phone call. When he said yes, I had my attorney sue the dean for malice.

If I won on the malice suit, the dean would not be covered by the university or his malpractice insurance. A loss, which was likely and perhaps probable, would wipe him out, eliminating all his personal assets. He caved. The university returned all the original funds to MacArthur and they restored to my budget the nearly million dollars that by then I had from MacArthur. But they refused to pay my legal costs. I was stuck with a legal bill of $15,000; not much to offset all the grant funds that were restored.

I acquired the reputation of a litigious person, not to be messed with, and I wasn't for a number of years.

During the 1980s and 1990s, about a third of my time was devoted to the experiments on deception and training various law enforcement groups. My colleagues often complained that I should not be training cops, whom they viewed as bad guys. I would reply "don't you want them to make less mistakes, putting less innocent people in jail?" That shut them up, but I knew many disapproved of this part of my work. When I received in 1991 the highest honor the American Psychological Association gives for research, and when in 1982 the faculty senate at UCSF awarded me the highest honor for the most important research by a faculty member that year, neither mentioned my research on lying, only the work on emotion.

It was not only that I was applying my work on lying to law enforcement, but also a prejudice against applied research in much of academia. I have often said that there are two unwritten rules in academic research: if it is useful it is not important; and, if a machine can do it then it is important. There is a new one recently: if what you study either focuses on the brain or can be related to brain structure, it is important.

I was unhappily spending a third of my time writing grants to the government and foundations to support my lab, and giving public presentations about my findings. Another third I spent overseeing the deception research and its application through training. The last third was devoted to my research on emotion, mostly closing loopholes, replicating findings, and always looking for money to support my lab.

At one point there were twenty-five people working in my lab, with separate teams headed by separate Ph.D.'s running one or another project. One project was on TV violence, another on emotion physiology, another on deception. I needed a few grants to maintain it. Even though the university put no money into my lab, taking money for overhead out instead, they kept promoting people, increasing their salaries, and the financial burden that imposed on me. Most important was to maintain the collaboration with Wally Friesen, who oversaw with great care every project and the work of all the research assistants.

I realized that I had become an idea man, a writer of findings, but my hands were no longer in the research itself. More than half of my time was consumed with writing grant proposals.

CHAPTER 20

The Network Television Show *Lie to Me*

I RECEIVED A PHONE CALL in 2006 from a fellow who said he was Brian Grazier's amanuensis, a fancy name for a personal assistant. Mr. Grazier wanted to meet me. Would I fly down to L.A. to discuss how they could make a TV show about my research on lie catching? The planes fly both ways, I replied, and if the topic was interesting my first hour was always free.

It was about five months before I heard from him again with the same plea, but my response was the same. By then I had Googled Grazier, whom I found had a large entry about his triumphs in both television (e.g., the show *24*) and cinema (e.g., *Titanic*). I had already had a lot of contact with broadcast TV, appearing on the *Tonight Show Starring Johnny Carson Show, Oprah,* a Bill Moyers special, *Good Morning America, 20/20, Dateline*—all about my book *Telling Lies.* No one had ever wanted to make entertainment TV about my work. While it sounded like fun, the likelihood of oversimplification or vulgarity worried me.

When, some months later, I had to be in Beverly Hills to see a friend, I let Grazier's office know I was available, which resulted in an hour's meeting at his less than opulent offices. Before I even sat down, Grazier, who had an odd appearance with very spiky stand-up hair, asked me why he couldn't get it up for his wife anymore. These Hollywood women, he said, were all too skinny. I told him I was not that kind of doctor! I was to later learn that Hollywood TV people think everyone will find their dirty underwear interesting.

Brian went on to flatter me about my fascinating research and how much he had enjoyed *Telling Lies*. He would be back in touch when he found the right writer.

It was another year before the amanuensis called, asking me to fly down to meet the writer, Sam Baum, and David Niven, the head of Brian's TV production studio. I insisted they fly up. Before the meeting date was set, Sam sent me the script for a play he had written. It was very impressive. He not only had talent, but I liked the subtlety and complexity. I was also taken with his appearance when we met—dressed informally, tall, skinny, with bright red hair. I took an instant liking to Sam. They told me they had been funded to make a pilot show, without having to go through the usual step of first submitting a script for approval. They wanted me to consult on the script, as they would want me to do on every show if a series was approved after the pilot was viewed.

Although flattered, I saw too great a likelihood that false information would be shown. I said I was not going to help them. They said they would do it with or without me. I had already provided enough for them in my writings and TV interviews. If I were to become part of the team I would get paid, not a great deal as it was to turn out, but enough to pay for a few overseas vacations every year. I would see every script a few weeks before it was shot. They would read my criticisms and suggestions, but they would not be obligated to follow what I said, only to consider it. I could also exclude ahead of time certain topics (in the contract with them I excluded anything about my work with the Dalai Lama). I also insisted that the actor they would be hiring to play the scientist could not be an American, married, have two children, or a personality similar to mine. I hoped by these stipulations to preserve some privacy. They hired the English actor Tim Roth.

I very much enjoyed the discussions with Sam Baum. The pilot program was in everyone's judgment very interesting and entertaining. The show was launched for a first season. I made many trips down to the 20th Century Fox studio. I met with the team of writers working under Sam's direction. He had required them to read *Telling Lies*, and they were full of questions. Talking with them was like running a very smart graduate academic seminar. I got to know the actors, all of whom I liked, even Tim Roth, whom I seemed to make nervous. I sometimes sat on the set while they shot part of a program, giving suggestions, showing them how to make a certain gesture or expression. It was fun. A different part of life from what I had known.

I found myself spending about eight hours a week on the show, and because that sometimes was not enough, I asked my former graduate student Erika Rosenberg to help me, which she was happy to do. We both made a video library of examples for the actors to study. But Sam did not always follow my advice, and sometimes provided false information, knowingly. In the very first show, for instance, one of the actors said people tell ten lies every day. Even though a fellow scientist had published such a claim, I had told Sam there was no way to know how many lies people told each day, unless you had an invisible cloak. But it was such a good line, he said, and really worked well in the story.

Yet, sometimes in less than a minute they made an idea I had spent pages trying to explain come alive, instantly understandable. For example, the fact that someone looks guilty doesn't mean they committed the crime you are investigating. People can be guilty about many matters; you need to find out what they are guilty about. I was delighted that they had so quickly and accurately got that idea across.

Another error happened when an athlete known as A-Rod wrongly performed an action that the show said was a sign of anger. It would be correct if he had thrust his jaw forward with his head level, but he did it pointing his jaw upwards. That doesn't happen.

Worst of all, the show made identifying who was lying sometimes too easy and too certain. In my experience, often it was neither. I told Sam about my worries. Someday someone who had watched *Lie to Me* might, if on a jury, mistakenly judge an innocent person to be lying. Sam won from Fox TV the opportunity for me to write a critique of each program. That appeared on Fox's own website, starting the day after each program was shown.

I called my weekly blog *The Truth about Lie to Me, Separating the Facts from the Fiction*. Sometimes I just further explained something that had been very brief on the show; often I pointed out a mistake. And, every blog opened with the warning:

Caveat: How the Lightman Group spots lies is largely based on findings from my research. Because it is a drama not a documentary, Dr. Lightman is not as tentative about interpreting behavior as I am. Lies are uncovered more quickly and with more certainty than it happens in reality. But most of what you see is based on scientific evidence. Each show also provocatively raises the complex psychological and ethical issues involved in perpetrating and uncovering lies. In this weekly BLOG I explain more about the science behind what you have been seeing and when the show takes poetic license.

Here are a couple of examples of my comments on a specific point in a show in the second season. The numbers that open each paragraph indicate how many minutes into the show before this event occurs:

[12:17] The FBI agent Ben says innocent people don't run. That is not always so. Innocent people run when they are convinced they will be wrongly judged, as is in the case here.

[25:07] After Torres makes the remark about Matthieson's wife having to clean up after his messes, Lightman says "that will do Torres," and shows a beautiful anger expression: brows lowered, glaring eyes, and most importantly, the upper lip narrowed and lower lip tightened.

[35:28] Mike, the guy who loaned the money and had the fling with Connie, is confronted with the tape recorder. Foster says "that's how it happened, isn't that right?" Mike replies, "no, that's not how it happened," but his voice is very soft. We have found that a sudden shift to *soft-voice* is suggestive that the person is lying.

I believe this was the first time a network TV company allowed a critic to comment on a show on the network's own website the day after it appeared. Perhaps it was because over time *The Truth about Lie to Me* developed millions of readers.

Around halfway through the first season I was emailed a script about an attempt to assassinate President Obama. I immediately wrote Sam Baum that they must not do it. From what I had heard through the grapevine there already were a large number of threats on the President. Such a show ran the danger of increasing that number. I heard nothing back for a week, which was unusual; I typically got a response within two days at most.

I thought of threatening to resign, but I had a contract, and I didn't want to get involved in a legal dispute. Instead, I contacted the director of the Secret Service, with whom I had a first name relationship, letting him know what was being planned and my attempt to stop it. If *Lie to Me* went ahead despite my advice, I would let the director know when the program would appear. I wrote Sam again, telling him what I had done and adding that the Secret Service hoped they would not use that story line. If *Lie to Me* did make such a show, the Secret Service would issue a press release the day it was shown criticizing the show. I told Sam I would also contact the people I knew at ABC TV telling them what was about to occur, offering to appear on their network criticizing *Lie To Me*'s poor judgment. After a tense week, a new script arrived about a threat against the secretary of agriculture.

When Tim Roth learned that the show would be renewed for another year, he said "this is a show about Dr. Lightman (the name of the scientist on the show), not Dr. Ekman! I don't want to do so much science." He didn't, and the show writers were not allowed to put much in. Sam Baum left the show for personal reasons at the end of the first year. Often my blogs read "no science, no comment." The ratings went down. The show got boring. By the end of the third year it was cancelled. I was relieved. It was still taking me eight hours a week to read dull scripts. On balance, I think *Lie to Me* probably did more harm than good, for the reasons I described earlier. But it raised interest in how demeanor might betray lies, in micro facial expressions, and in me as a public person.

CHAPTER 21

Loose Ends

RESEARCH

I NEVER PUBLISHED a number of interesting findings. Sometimes it was because I just didn't have the time to do so, as it is not a simple matter to put what you discover into the restrained language scientific journals require, and then to deal with the hidden anonymous reviewers. (I have always insisted that my identity be revealed when I have been a reviewer, so the author could question whether I was unbiased.) Nearly every article I submitted to a scientific journal was initially rejected. I then would write counterarguments, eventually succeeding, but it usually took nearly two years after initial submission of an article to get it accepted, then usually another year before it appeared in print.

Some projects I never completely finished once I knew the answer, moving on to something else, most often giving priority to writing still another grant to support my lab. I didn't have graduate students to delegate the task of completing projects or writing them up (that was the cost of being a faculty member in a medical school unrelated to a department of psychology). Often I didn't have the motivation to try to get a grant to pay the costs of repeating a study, as I rarely published anything I had not repeated. Once I knew the answer to a question, although I wanted to share it, I didn't want to invest the time necessary to do so. I instead I put my time into publishing the findings that were likely to get grants renewed.

BLINDED BY FRIENDSHIP. In one of my early studies in the 1970s of deception, I compared the accuracy of friends with strangers in judging when someone was lying or telling the truth. To my initial surprise strangers were more accurate! I interpreted this unexpected finding as due to friends trusting their friends. If you suspected your friend was lying, the friendship would not be likely to continue. Friendship, and other intimate relationships, requires trust. Trust makes you vulnerable to being exploited or betrayed. This is consistent with the common observation that the cuckold is the last to recognize the betrayal, well after the lies of the betraying lover were obvious to others.

We unwittingly avoid information that would disconfirm our trust. We don't want to find out our children are lying about use of hard drugs, any more than we want to know the person we recommended for a job is embezzling. Rationally, we need to know; psychologically, we don't. Most lies succeed, I believe, because the target unwittingly cooperates in being duped.

RACE AND SEX BIAS ON PERCEPTION OF FACES. Randy Harrison was a professor on leave from Michigan State University, working with me on the television violence projects, and he stayed to work on other matters. We investigated how sexual and racial bias influenced the recognition of emotion. We traced onto acetate sheets (note the very old pre-digital technology) the prototypical expressions of the seven universal emotions. Then we produced other acetate overlays showing a Caucasian male hairdo; African American hair; and a Caucasian female hairstyle. We didn't know how to signal an African American female with hairstyling.

These images were shown for a fraction of a second to college students, who had to judge which emotion they had seen and the intensity of the emotion. Neither sex nor race influenced the judgment of which emotion they had seen, but the strength of the emotion differed. Anger was judged more intense when shown by an African American male as compared to a Caucasian male. Fear and sadness were judged more intense when shown by a female than male Caucasian. Those findings were the same for the Caucasians and African Americans who saw the facial expressions. We never took the next step to find out what might be the correlates of the extent of prejudice shown.

MORE ACCURATE RATINGS OF SUBJECTIVE EMOTIONAL EXPERIENCE. I enlisted the aid of the late Maureen O'Sullivan, a close friend and collaborator in many of my deception studies, in a methodological study of self-ratings of felt emotion. The typical procedure, which is still widely used today, is to give people scales from 1 to 7 (or 9), to rate how intensely they felt each emotion, after having undergone some emotional experience. The problem I saw in such an approach is that different people might have very different ideas in mind about what is represented by the endpoint number 7. I might rate my experience of fear as a 5 because I was thinking 7 stood for fear of impending death, while another person might rate their experience as 5 thinking that 7 stood for fear felt in a good horror movie. If I had known that 7 stood for the fear felt in a horror movie, I would have rated my fear as 6 or 7, not 5, but I imagined 7 to be fear of impending death. I thought that if asked directly people would agree that the horror movie fear is not as strong as the fear of impending death. The problem arises because the endpoint of the scale is never defined but left up to the imagination of the responder, and different people imagine different endpoints.

The remedy, we thought, was to define the anchor point for the most extreme point on the scale, what the 7 stands for. To accomplish this, we asked a group of people to write down what they imagined the most extreme fear (anger, sadness, etc.) anyone in the world had ever felt. Interestingly we found that it was the same for anger and fear: threat of immediate physical harm to self or family. We obtained high agreement about what they imagined would be the most extreme experience of each of the other emotions: death of a child for sadness; unexpected windfall of money for surprise; stepping into animal feces for disgust; unfortunately, I can't find what we discovered for happiness and I can't remember it.

With this data we could define what a 7 stood for, anchoring it in a specific experience. With that remedy we eliminated variations in what people imagined, and everyone used the same scale with the same endpoint defined for them.

I still regret that we never published what we called AnchorQ, but we would have had to do research using the usual seven-point scales as compared to an anchored seven-point scale, and show a difference in relationship to expression or physiology. I think we would have done so, but it would take more work and writing a grant to fund it, so it fell by the wayside.

FACIAL MUSCULAR TENSION AND EXPRESSION. When I was exploring how the facial muscles worked, I noticed that I could tense a muscle very strongly without producing any visible facial expression. How activated the muscle becomes does not determine whether or not it pulls the skin to which it is attached to generate a visible expression. The conventional view was just the opposite, that the amount of tension in the muscle would directly translate into the strength of the facial expression it generated.

A popular method for measuring facial expressions at that time was to attach electrodes to the surface of the face, measuring the amount of electrical activity in different facial regions. It was a fast method, not taking anywhere near the amount of time that measurement with our Facial Action Coding System (FACS) required. If I was right, it called into question the use of what was called EMG (electromyography) to measure expression. It was not equal to or a substitute for measuring facial expressions, for electrical activity does not always produce expressions. Another problem is that in some regions of the face muscles are layered on top of each other, making it impossible for EMG to reveal which muscle is producing the change in electrical activity.

I contacted Gary Schwartz, a young professor at Harvard, who was the most active person doing facial EMG, asking him to collaborate in a study to see if I was right in my claim that electrical activity did not distinguish between tense muscular activity that did and did not produce a facial expression. He expressed interest, and I and one of my most facially agile students at the time, Harriet Oster, traveled to his lab in Boston. With Gary's electrodes pasted on our faces we generated what we thought were high levels of facial muscular tension with no visible change in appearance.

Despite repeated requests Gary did not analyze the EMG recordings. Only now do I wonder whether his reluctance might have been motivated by a wish not to prove that his favorite method of research was not measuring what it claimed to measure.

When I was working in Gary's lab to generate the tense facial muscular activity without expression, I met one of his graduate students, Richie Davidson. Richie offered to analyze the data, which showed what I had predicted—you could not tell from EMG measurement whether or not there was a facial expression, only that there was tension in a group of muscles. I reported that in a chapter in a book I co-edited on methods for measuring nonverbal behavior.

But the real benefit was meeting Richie, who over the next years obtained his Ph.D. at Harvard, set up a lab at SUNY Purchase, and then became a full professor at Wisconsin. Richie became a very close personal friend, and a collaborator on studies in the 1990s that verified what distinguishes a genuine smile of enjoyment (what I called a Duchenne smile in honor of the French neuroscientist who first proposed what it would be) from a social smile.

Many years later Richie was a participant in the meeting when I first met the Dalai Lama, and then helped me put together the Cultivating Emotional Balance project, which I organized in response to the Dalai Lama's challenge of whether this meeting with a group of scientists would just be talk or would actually lead to something concrete. Richie now runs the largest lab in the world studying the neuroscience of meditation and compassion. Although I don't get to see him as often as I would like, I feel he is my younger brother.

Through Richie, I met Cliff Saron, who was Richie's lab manager at Purchase and then Wisconsin. Some years later, Cliff earned his Ph.D. in neuroscience, and recently ran the largest, most complete, and most complex study on the impact of meditation. Cliff is a perfectionist, worse than me in that regard, a techy, an insightful thinker, a methodologist without peer. He has a position at Davis and lives in the Bay Area, so I get to see him often, and rely on his advice on matters scientific, bureaucratic, and ethical. And, to close the circle, he is now providing mentorship to the young, pretty Dr. Ekman, my daughter, Eve.

GENES AND FACIAL EXPRESSIONS. Thomas Bouchard, professor of psychology at the University of Minnesota, invited me to participate (along with some noteworthy colleagues at Minnesota) in his study of twins reared apart from birth. The study had been underway for some time when he offered this extraordinary opportunity. He was in the midst of investigating a large group of identical and fraternal twins who had been reared apart from birth, through adoption, in separate families. Most of the twins were adult to middle-aged by the time Bouchard found them, unaware that they had a twin.

Bouchard agreed to show each twin two of my emotionally arousing films: a film (I had shot myself) of my puppy playing with a flower and a film of an industrial accident, used by me and many previous investigators. Video of their facial expressions was recorded with a hidden camera, and they self-reported emotion on both rating scales and in a brief interview. I watched the first pair of identical twins who still had not met each other, as each one went through my procedure.

I didn't have the time to get a grant to pay for someone to work on this. I recently wrote to Kenneth Kendler, M.D. (University of Virginia), who worked on the videos and published a report, asking him how it came about. I now quote from his email responding to my query:

> *I was interested in new ways to assess emotions in twins that did not rely on self-report. I heard from Tom Bouchard about his collaboration with you on the facial expressions and that the data had never been analyzed. That led me to contact you and get the tapes. Rating the tapes was very effortful, and it would have been hard to scale it up to the 100s of twins needed to have statistical power. Also, the results we obtained—in terms of twin resemblances—not very robust. The sample was small but it seemed to me that the [emotions being experienced] probably were also very important for some of these measures.*

Tom Bouchard recently emailed me:

> *Kendler was not able to make use of a number of them because the recorder did not work properly, that is why the*

sample size is so small. . . . I know for a fact that some of the videos are pretty bad as they were not kept at proper room temperature.

Nevertheless Kendler's findings that duration was a more useful measure than the magnitude of an expression, and that there was more evidence of a genetic influence for spontaneous as compared to posed expressions is useful. The lesson also is that, if you want work to be done, you have to hang around and monitor the recordings as they are being made, and later how they are stored. I couldn't do that because I didn't write a grant application to pay for someone to be on-site and look after the recordings

INDIVIDUAL EMOTIONAL PROFILES. I wrote the grant that obtained the funding to collaborate with Bob Levenson in collecting a unique data set to answer the following three questions about emotion:

1. To what extent are emotional reactions specific to how the emotion is aroused? Is my theory correct that once triggered, the reaction is the same regardless of how it was triggered? For example, if you become angry by news about some event you read about in the newspaper or angry at your child, the impulses generated in each instance will result in largely similar changes in expression and autonomic nervous system activity. My theory is that emotional responses are generated by an affect program, which contains innate and learned instructions for the responses for each emotion. Once the affect program is triggered, it sends out impulses to

physiology and expression, I think, regardless of how it was triggered.

In order to answer this question we triggered each emotion in three quite different tasks: viewing emotionally arousing films, remembering a past intense emotional experience, and my directed facial action task, in which people were coached in how to voluntarily produce each emotional facial expression. The answer to the first question is that the type of change produced in physiology and expression is the same, regardless of how the emotion was triggered.

2. Are the changes in physiology, expression, and self-reported experience coherent or independent of each other? If you show a large or small response on one set of measures, such as heart rate for example, will you also show the same magnitude in the facial muscle contractions? The answer is yes, you will.

3. Are there stable individual differences in the speed of response and strength of response, evident in all three measures—facial muscle contractions, changes in autonomic nervous system physiology, and self-reported subjective experience? The answer is yes.

Because I was unable to get a grant to analyze the data (I won't bother to describe why), I had to do the analysis slowly with pirated funds. By the time it was completed I had begun to plan my retirement from UCSF and close my laboratory, which had been active for thirty-five years.

What was most important to me was the support in the findings for the idea that people differ in what I called their *emotional profile*. Some people consistently respond quickly, others more slowly; some people usually have large responses, others have smaller ones. I am not just referring to the strength and speed of their facial expressions, but the changes in autonomic nervous system activity and self-reported experience as well!

The emotional profile for enjoyment is radically different from the profile for anger, fear, disgust, and sadness. These seem to be two independent systems. Furthermore, I saw hints in the data of two more characteristics of an individual's emotional profile: in addition to speed and magnitude, which I had measured, there are likely to be stable differences in the duration of an emotional response and the time it takes to recover and return to a baseline emotional state.

I propose that people know their own emotional profiles, but don't have a way of organizing their thinking about it. Those we are intimately involved with also know our emotional profiles. I am currently developing a tool that will allow people to chart their profile, and then compare their chart with how an intimate partner charts their profile.

ATTEMPTS TO CREATE RESEARCH INSTITUTES. Charles Darwin Institute:

In the early 1980s I tried to create a research institute that would be capable of pursuing the leads that Darwin had described in his great book on expression, which would include examining emotion across cultures and developmental changes across the life span, in humans and at least chimpanzees. If I could get the funds to support what I called the Charles Darwin Center for the Study of Emotion for ten years I had commitments from Klaus Scherer for the voice, Richie Davidson for the central nervous system, Bob Levenson for the autonomic nervous system, and my group for the face—all to be housed at the Darwin Center engaging in collaborative research. I do think they would have come, as at that time they were all assistant professors without tenure. The opportunity for unique collaborations and the freedom from grant writing for ten years was very seductive.

The budget I wrote up in the proposal also included support for three-year fellowships for scientists' expert on children and on chimpanzees, as well as a number of postdoctoral fellowships. The budget for this grant proposal was over 15 million dollars. I sent it to a number of foundations. Sloan Foundation showed interest, asking for more information, and then more. They opened the door, asked me to sit down, asked me in again, and then told me they had decided instead to support cognitive science. So, it never happened; almost, but never.

Max Planck Institute:

In the late 1960s and '70s I often visited the Max Planck Institute in Munich, as well as an offshoot institute outside of Munich run by Irenäus Eibl-Eibesfeldt, where he stored and did some analysis of his ethnographic films. These people were the intellectual descendants of the famous German scientist Konrad Lorenz, and despite the fact that I did not think *imprinting* existed in humans, a Lorenzian term for how early exposure to a mothering figure would permanently establish that figure as the mother in the infant's mind, they were very receptive to my cross-cultural studies of expression when most American psychologists were not.

In the late 1980s they asked me if I would like to head up a new Max Planck Institute in San Francisco. I would have lifetime support for myself plus four or five support personnel, including some at a Ph.D. level. I would also be responsible for recruiting four or five more such groups of scientists. Only one condition: Eibl-Eibesfeldt had to be head of one of those groups, moving his group from Munich to San Francisco. I said I would gladly accept if Eibl wanted to move; he didn't, and so it never happened.

MISCELLANY

JURY INSTRUCTIONS. In the late 1980s and early 1990s, I was invited to talk to judges, at both state and federal gatherings. I spoke mainly about how the courtroom seemed to have been designed to make it very difficult to evaluate credibility. One of my contributions was to critique the federal instructions to juries, which many judges relied upon, and to provide a better set of instructions based on current research:

COMMENTS ON PROBLEMS IN THE CURRENT FEDERAL INSTRUCTIONS TO JURIES

You as jurors are the sole judges of the credibility of the witnesses and the weight their testimony deserves. You may be guided by the appearance and conducted of the witness, or by the manner in which the witness testifies, or by the character of the testimony given, or by evidence to the contrary of the testimony given. . . . Consider each witness's intelligence, motive, and state of mind and demeanor or manner while on stand.

From *Manual of Model Jury Instructions for the Ninth Circuit*

PROBLEMS:

Appearance: Probably the most misleading and a source of stereotyping. Juries should be told to disregard appearance, to guard against our natural tendency to disbelieve those who are unattractive or whose dress and appearance is unconventional.

Manner: Manner can be very misleading. Juries need to be warned about being influence by personal mannerisms or idiosyncrasies. Very truthful people may be restless, tense, or nervous when they testify.

Conduct: This is an old-fashioned word, but not a bad one. Jurors should be told to consider not just what the witness says, but how they say it—expressions, gestures, posture, and tone of voice. Focus on changes in demeanor with a change in what the witness is asked about.

PROPOSED INSTRUCTIONS TO JURIES ABOUT JUDGING CREDIBILITY

You as jurors are the sole judges of the credibility of the witnesses and the weight their testimony deserves. You may be guided by the character of the testimony given or by evidence

to the contrary of the testimony given. Consider each wit-
ness's intelligence, motive, state of mind, and demeanor
while on the stand.[1]

Try not to be swayed by the appearance of the witness, the
clothing, hairstyle, or grooming. Guard against the natural
tendency to believe people whose appearance is similar to
your own dress and grooming.[2] Also be on guard against
being influenced by how attractive the witness may be.[3]
Beware of an inclination to be more sympathetic to a wit-
ness who is appealing in his or her appearance. These factors
are often unrelated to a witness's truthfulness.

Mannerisms can also be misleading. Sometimes a truthful
witness may seem to be nervous or tense. Such a witness
may be intimidated by the courtroom, and some witnesses
are typically nervous, fidgety, or tense in their manner.[4]

Evaluate not just what the witness says, but how the wit-
ness says it. Pay attention to the facial expressions, gestures,
posture, and tone of voice. Look for discrepancies between
what the witness says and how the witness says it. But
remember that sometimes truthful witnesses may look wor-
ried if they are afraid of being disbelieved, and some liars
can behave very convincingly.[5]

---

[1] This wording is unchanged from the *Manual of Model Jury Instructions for the Ninth Circuit*, except that I deleted the following from it: "You may be guided by the appearance . . . or by the manner in which the witness testifies." The rest of the text that follows is new.

[2] G. R. Miller and J. K. Burgoon, "Factors affecting assessments of witness credibility. A chapter in R. Bray and N. L. Kerr (editors), *The Psychology of the Courtroom*. New York: Academic Press, 1982.

I talked to many judges about the need to provide those instructions at the beginning of a trial, not the end, so jurors would have them in mind when they observed testimony, rather than being told how to evaluate testimony often long after it was given. That reform, I was frustrated to learn, never was adopted.

INTERPRETING THE SMILE OF A PRISON GUARD. *Was it the Smile of a Ghoul?*

I long admired Errol Morris, and when his film *The Fog of War* was screened at Berkeley I introduced myself to him after the discussion of the film was over. He knew my work and was quite friendly. A few years later he asked me if I would evaluate photographs of Sabrina Harman, who had been a military guard in the prison Abu Ghraib. I quote now from what Morris used in his book *Believing Is Seeing:*

Is Sabrina a good or a bad person? You tell me. She was part of the nightmare of abuse at Abu Ghraib, but her own act of

---

[3] M. G. Efran, "The effect of physical appearance on the judgment of guilt, interpersonal attraction, and severity of recommended punishment in a simulated jury task." *Journal of Research in Personality,* 8, pages 45–54, 1974.

[4] A number of research studies that support this are described in: Paul Ekman, *Telling Lies,* second Edition, New York: W. W. Norton, 2001. Also see, Paul Ekman, Maureen O'Sullivan, W. V. Friesen, and Klaus Scherer, "Face, voice and body in detecting deception." *Journal of Nonverbal Behavior,* 15.

[5] Paul Ekman and Maureen O'Sullivan. "Who Can Catch A Liar." *American Psychologist,* 1991, 46, 913–920.

defiance, her act of civil disobedience, was to take these photographs, to provide proof of what others were trying to deny. But her smile still made me feel uneasy. And I was not alone. The New York Post *headline characterized her as "The Ghoul Next Door." In the trial of public perception Sabrina Harman was guilty. Her photographs and the photographs in which she appeared proved it. How are we to interpret her expression?*

It was because of my continuing uneasiness with the smile that I contacted Paul Ekman, [professor] emeritus of psychology at the University of California, San Francisco. I contacted him despite my uneasiness with "smile science." Ekman is an expert on facial expression and has written many books, including Emotions Revealed, Unmasking the Face, *and* Telling Lies. *He also had an extremely popular television show,* Lie to Me, *on Fox [it was not my show but a show I consulted on]. I asked him if he could explain Sabrina's smile.*

I sent him a CD with over twenty pictures of Sabrina Harman, including the thumbs up picture of Sabrina with al-Jamadi's corpse. It is labeled picture 2728.

Paul Ekman: *In picture 2728 she is showing a social smile or a smile for the camera. The signs of an actual enjoyment smile are just not there. She's doing what people always do when* they pose for the camera, they put on a big, broad smile, but they're not actually enjoying themselves. We would see movement in the eye cover fold [if she was truly enjoying herself]. That's the area of the

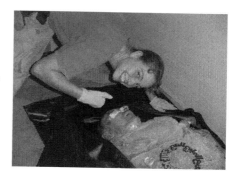

skin below the eyebrow before the eyelid. And it moves slightly down only with genuine enjoyment. In one of her pictures I get a chance to see her with no emotion on her face. That's picture 4034. So I can see what the eye cover fold looks like when she's not smiling. And it's just the same as with the smile. That's

the crucial difference between what I call a Duchenne smile, the true smile of enjoyment named after the French neurologist who first made the discovery in 1862, and the forced smile, the social smile.

Errol Morris: *So 4034 is the comparison picture?*

Paul Ekman: *Yes. That's the picture I used for comparison. She's getting something out of a box and has a black beanie on her head. Okay? If you go back to the first picture, 2728, and you look at the eye cover fold on that one, if it was an enjoyment smile, the amount of skin between the upper eye lid and the brow would be considerably reduced. We've got a lot of data on that and some published articles. It's the clue. It's a fairly subtle clue most people don't attend to. But it's the only reliable clue that the muscle called the* orbicularis oculi, pars lateralis *isn't activated. It's an involuntary muscle. It only gets activated in nearly all people when there's genuine enjoyment.*

Errol Morris: *And you don't see that in Sabrina's smile?*

Paul Ekman: *No, It's just what people put on their face when someone's going to take a photograph of them, a big, broad smile. The crucial thing is, there's no sign she's really feeling genuine enjoyment while this picture's being taken. Nor is there any sign she feels any other emotion, no sign of sadness, no fear, no disgust, and no contempt. It's just a 'say cheese' smile.*

Errol Morris: *It makes me think the 'say cheese' smile was invented for photography.*

Paul Ekman: *Oh, no, no. people do this all the time. This is a very broad smile. It's the* zygomaticus *major. That's the muscle that pulls the lip corners up obliquely. And she's contracted it to its maximum. In the typical polite smile you give a host for dinner party, when you're going home, and telling them you really enjoyed yourself, but you didn't, you would employ the same* zygomaticus *muscle, but it wouldn't be as contracted as much. It would be inappropriate to give this broad a smile for most polite smiles. This broad a smile only occurs with genuine enjoyment or when you're posing for a camera.*

Errol Morris: *Just once again, so I can be sure I understand. You can distinguish the 'say cheese' smile from genuine smiling, the smile of enjoyment.*

Paul Ekman: *Absolutely. It's the absence of the* orbicularis oculi, pars lateralis. *That muscle orbits the eye completely. It pulls up the cheek, and it produces crow's feet wrinkles. However when you get a broad smile, like she's doing, that pushes the cheeks up anyhow. And it will produce crow's feet wrinkles just on their own. So the only reliable clue as to whether* orbicularis oculi, pars lateralis *has acted is to look above the eye. No muscle can lower that skin other than the* orbicularis oculi. *The smiling muscle,* zygomaticus, *can't affect it. So you can put on as big a smile as you want and the cover fold skin will not come down.*

Errol Morris: *I should tell you why I'm asking all these questions.*

Paul Ekman: *Yes I'm curious.*

Errol Morris: *I've just finished this movie on the Abu Ghraib photographs. And I believe many of the photographs have been misunderstood for many reasons and in many different ways. The picture of Sabrina Harman smiling with her thumb up above the body of Iraqi prisoner, we know his name, Manadel al-Jamadi. People saw this picture and were horrified. They took her smile as a smile of enjoyment, a smile of pleasure.*

Paul Ekman: *So what's the explanation of why she has the smile and the thumbs up?*

Errol Morris: *Her explanation is that she did it all the time. People would take her picture, and she would have the same goofy smile and the same thumbs up, again and again and again and again.*

Paul Ekman: *Well, there are a lot of them.*

Errol Morris: *I often think about Sabrina being a woman, a gay woman in the military, trying to show that she is in command, a master of her emotions, not cowed by her experiences but in control. Of course, when they see the photograph they do not see Sabrina. They see the smile.*

Paul Ekman: *Well here's what I think happens when the typical viewer looks at the picture: one, you're horrified by the sight of the dead person. Most of us haven't seen a dead person certainly not in that state. If you've seen a dead person, you've seen them in an open casket where they're made to look like they're alive. Do you know how the word* horror *is defined?*

Errol Morris: *Tell me.*

Paul Ekman: *'Horror,' according to the* Oxford English Dictionary, *is the combination of disgust and terror. So I think horror is the right word. It's a horrible sight and it instills horror. And then you see right next to that someone having a good time. Most people will not realize that's a 'say cheese' smile. They'll think, because of the broadness of the smile and the thumbs up gesture, they're having a good time. That's what makes this a damning picture to the typical viewer. I'll add one more thing. When we see someone smile its almost irresistible that we smile back at them. Advertisers know this. They link products to smiling faces. And when we smile back, we begin to actually experience some enjoyment. So this photograph makes us complicit in enjoying the horrible. And that's revolting to us.*

Here is Ekman's explanation: it's not an upsetting photograph just because we see some smiling in the context of the horrible, but because when we look at her, we have to resist smiling ourselves. We see her smiling and start to smile ourselves. But when we see the dead man we recoil in horror. Our 'almost irresistible' need to smile makes us feel complicit in the man's death. And it makes us angry. We 'transfer' those feelings to Sabrina.

In a letter written by Sabrina to Kelly, her wife, four days after al-Jamadi's death she writes about her "fake smile." Many people have read the letter and assumed either the letter is a forgery, that it was written long after the fact, or it was written opportunistically to put herself in a better light. I don't believe either claim. Many of the letters were postmarked from Abu Ghraib. Many of them (including the letter below) were not submitted into evidence at Sabrina's court martial, and it was only after much negotiation with Sabrina that I was able to see them and publish them. The letters are invaluable because they provide an emotional context for the photographs that is not available through any other source.

Kelly,

I'm not sure how to feel. I have a lot of anxiety, I think something is going to happen either with me not making it or you doing something wrong. I think too much. I hope I'm wrong but if not, know that I love you, and you are and will always be my wife. I hate being so scared. I hate anxiety. I hate the unknown. We might be under investigation. I AM NOT SURE, THERE'S TALK ABOUT IT. Yes, they beat up the prisoners and I've written this to you before. I just don't think it's right and never have. That's why I take the pictures to prove the story I tell people. No one would believe the shit that goes on. No one. The dead guy didn't bother me, even took a picture with him doing thumbs up. But that's when I realized it wasn't funny anymore, that this guy had blood in his nose. I didn't even have to check his ears and I already knew it was not a heart attack they claimed he died of. He bled to death from some cause of trauma to his head. I was told when they took him out they put an IV and put him on a stretcher like he was alive to fool the people around they said the autopsy came back "heart attack." It's a lie. The whole military is nothing but lies. They cover up too much. The guy was never in our prison that's the story. The fucked up thing is we never touched the guy. As soon as they released him to us, he died only a few minutes later, if I want to keep taking pictures of those events I even have short films I have to fake smiles every time. I hope I don't get in trouble for something I haven't done. I hate this. I hate being away from home and I hate half the people I'm surrounded by. They're idiots. I can't be here. I don't want to be a part of the army, because it makes me one of them. I don't like it here. I don't like what we do.

When the army was looking for a scapegoat for its crimes it was precisely this smiling image of Sabrina they used to their advantage. And thus Sabrina Harman's photographs became part of the evidence used against her in military court and in the court of public opinion.

Seymour Hersh wrote in the *New Yorker*, "These photographs tell it all." But they do not. We don't learn in Hersh's article that al-Jamadi was not killed by the MPs. The photographs are the start of a trail of evidence, but not the end.

From the date Abu Ghraib photographs were first made public to the present time, very little has been written to clarify the relationship between the photographs and what happened that night. We see al-Jamadi's body, but we don't see the homicidal act that turned him from a human being into a corpse. We don't understand what the photograph means nor what is it about. Instead of asking Who is this man? Who killed him? The question becomes "Why is this women smiling?" At first I believed that Sabrina was complicit in al-Jamadi's death. I was wrong: I too, was fooled by the smile.

And so we are left with a simple conundrum. Photographs reveal and they conceal. The photograph of Sabrina smiling over al-Jamadi's body both reveals his death and conceals his killer. We know about al-Jamadi's death because of Sabrina Harman. Without her photographs, his death would likely have been covered up by the CIA and the military. Sabrina didn't murder al-Jamadi. Nor did she try to conceal his death. She provided evidence of a crime, evidence that this was no heart attack victim. She took photographs to show that, as she put it, "the whole military is nothing but lies" or at the very least, to show she had been lied to by her commanding officer.

It should be our job to make sure that her photographs are used to prosecute the people truly responsible for al-Jamadi's death. The terrible truth is that the terrible torture techniques that killed al-Jamadi were authorized by the highest levels of government, but none of the myriad of investigations into al-Jamadi's death probed this fact. Were there other deadly interrogations? Deaths that we don't know about because they weren't photographed? We should demand accountability for the policies that allowed this murder and attempted to cover it up.

We shouldn't allow what happened at Abu Ghraib to disappear except for a smile. And like *Alice in Wonderland* we shouldn't be afraid to ask questions.

UNEXPECTED SOURCE STOPS MY LAB FROM CLOSING BECAUSE FUNDING RAN OUT: Earlier (page 103–104) I described how a totally unexpected and unsolicited source of funds rescued me from having to close my lab when Lionel Tiger and Robin Fox sought me out giving me the funds to complete the creation of the Facial Action Coding System (FACS). Another unexpected and unsolicited source of support came from the retired financier George Sarlo. Rabbi Steven Pearse was on the board of Sarlo's foundation and told George about my work. Pearse had come to know me when I briefly became a member of his congregation so that my daughter Eve could get bat mitzvahed. (She now considers herself a Buddhist, but then wanted to be Jewish, I suspect so she could have a big party as her age mates were having.) Sarlo took an interest in me and my research, and on his own initiative endowed the Sarlo-Ekman chair on human emotion research at UCSF. The first occupant of that chair is the well-known emotion researcher Wendy Mendes.

SENIOR GOVERNMENT OFFICIAL ASKS ME FOR ADVICE: One morning in 2003 a young woman telephoned asking if I would be able to meet with Scooter Libby the next time I was in Washington. (I didn't yet know that people high up in government rarely called someone they didn't already know. Instead they had intermediaries make the initial arrangements.) I knew who Scooter was; one newspaper had said Scooter was to Vice President Cheney what Cheney was to President Bush. I didn't like the policies of either Bush or Cheney, finding Cheney's public comments even more distasteful than those by Bush. But a door had opened and I was not going to let it close.

In response to my question asking what Scooter wished to talk about, I was told that I would find out when we met, the agenda was open, to be discovered during the meeting. I didn't like that answer but went along as the chance to meet with someone so high up in government had never come before and might not come again.

Within two weeks I flew to Washington and went to Scooter's office. I was impressed with the number of young female and male recent college graduates milling about in his outer office who referred to him as Scooter not Mr. Libby. I liked the informality so apparent in their manner of addressing him, and in the general tone of the place. Scooter himself was engaging, low key, appealing in his manner. After thanking me for coming to see him he asked if I had any suggestions about what the government could do to make America safer.

I was astounded. And more importantly grateful for the opportunity to tell him I knew of five things we could and should do. I can't remember all of them now but I expect they included: (1) training government security personnel in how to spot concealed emotions from micro facial expressions; (2) dangerous expressions, the facial appearance that immediately precedes a physical assault; and (3) the symbolic gestures relevant to possible assaults such as "'get out of here'", "'do it quickly'", watch out!'" Since my research found these gestures are not universal but specific to culture, nation or ethnic grouping, security personnel would have to learn the relevant symbolic gestures for each group that was hostile to the United States. I can't remember the other approaches I advocated, but I do remember that the three listed were the most important.

Scooter asked me to work up a budget and time line for accomplishing the work I had described and he would then arrange for me to meet "the speaker." "Mr. Hassert?" I asked; "No," he said "Newt Gingrich, who although no longer in office had his fingers on where the money is." A few weeks later I returned to Washington to meet with Mr. Gingrich for an appointment arranged by Scooter. Sitting in his waiting room I learned that Gingrich and

Hillary Clinton were working together to develop a health-care plan; I don't believe anything ever came from that collaboration.

Gingrich was tall, portly, and very well dressed. He seemed very smart from the questions he asked of me. He said he could find the funds for these projects if I could return with the names of who would lead each project (as I couldn't lead all of them), how long it would take, and what it would cost. I took up the challenge ready to return within a month, but by then Scooter was immersed in a scandal, in which I suspect he was taking the blame and the legal punishment, including being disbarred, for crimes that may have been Gingrich's, not his, or at least undertaken by Scooter at Gingrich's request.

But this is all supposition. Newt escaped without a blemish and Scooter was convicted of perjury when he denied having leaked the name of a CIA undercover agent whose husband had publicly denounced a project favored by Newt. It was a good lesson for me about the tangled politics of Washington. With Scooter now radio-active, Newt wanted nothing more to do with me, even though by then I had the information he had asked me to prepare for each of the projects he had earlier thought he would support.

A few years later I was having dinner at a well-known Washington restaurant with some Secret Service agents that I was working with when I saw Newt a few tables away. Also at his table were five very beautiful young women. I could not resist trying to embarrass him in front of his bevy by asking what he had heard from Scooter recently. I got a quick brushoff.

CHAPTER 22

Why I Closed My Lab and Retired from UCSF

THERE WERE MANY REASONS, intellectual, bureau-cratic, and personal, for my closing the lab. Running a lab is what I had done with my life, and being able to pursue the questions that interested me was what I wanted and was able to do for more than forty years. I was further enabled by a succession of career awards, five-year stipends that originally were equal to my salary from the university. These awards were intended to prevent senior scientists from being distracted by administration and teaching.

The terms of the Career Scientist Award, which the university had to accept, stipulated that I never be required to serve on any administrative committee, and that I not teach more than 20 percent of my time and then only about my own work. I always donated the money from these awards to my department. As I was freed from obligations other professors had to fulfill, it seemed proper to give those funds to the department rather than add it to my salary from the university, which I was free to do. In my early sixties, when I got my seventh award, I realized that it was unlikely I would get another when it ran out. I increasingly had the sense it was time to go.

When I started out, getting my first grant funded in 1963, half of the submissions were funded, and for almost thirty years with few exceptions everything I submitted was granted. Then the culture of reviewing changed. Established scientists with a very good track record were often not funded on new applications, but had to revise and resubmit the grants, a two-year process. I was spoiled; I had never had to do that before, and I wasn't willing to do it going forward.

Another change was that the reviewers, people like me (for five years I served on a review committee), no longer funded interesting ideas and a well-thought-out research plan. You had to have already done part of the research to show it would work. That was not what I had done for nearly thirty years, and I was not willing to change. I thought it was wrong to expect such proof of concept and feasibility of a research plan in advance of funding. Who was supposed to support that work? Such a policy would discourage scientists from taking risks. Also, it would be deadly to those whose salary depended on getting grants funded. My salary was on what is called "hard money," a tenured professorship. But nearly 90 percent of the faculty at the medical school lived from grant to grant or on patient fees. I wasn't willing to get the proof that my research plan would be productive. I was accustomed to getting the funds without having to do that.

Having a group of people working with me for many years was great, but the cost was that their salaries kept being raised by the university (which would not have to pay those salaries!), so that by the late 1990s I had to raise about $200,000 a year just for the salaries, apart from the other costs of the research.

The disagreement that caused our breakup was provoked by my challenging some very personal life choices that my associate Wally Friesen was making. It really wasn't my business, but we were more than research colleagues—we were also very close friends, used to giving each other advice about how we led our personal lives. But this time it didn't work, and the separation, the divorce, if you like, was bitter. He retired and moved across the country, and for a few years we had no contact.

He had to prove that he could do research without me, and he did; I had to prove that I could run my lab without him, and I did. After a few years we resumed contact, and have seen each other many times and have a warm friendship once again. The focus of our attention now is how to preserve the use of FACS when we are gone. That falls on me totally as Wally has recently died.

Another contributing factor to my decision to retire was the increasingly intrusive university requirements. When I started out there were no committees that reviewed your research to ensure you were protecting the rights of the people you studied. I had always taken precautions to do that. When I was studying psychiatric inpatients, I not only got their consent at the outset, but I asked them to renew their consent once they had been discharged. There were two reasons for doing this. When they were just admitted to the hospital, they were mentally disturbed and might not be able to accurately evaluate what was in their best interests. Also, they might fear that if they did not give consent they would not receive the best treatment for their disorder. So I took this precaution of contacting them after discharge and renewing their consent. My policy was never required by the university's review committee. One of the many reasons I regarded that review as just another unnecessary hurdle to jump, distracting me from doing the research.

My consent forms were quite elaborate, offering a menu of choices from maximum privacy, in which no one else other than my research team could see the films, to allowing their use in teaching, and specifying consents for different students (college, medical, or psychiatric only). At the extreme was choosing to consent to having the recordings shown on broadcast television. None of the psychiatric patients consented to this, but some of the people who participated in my research on deception did. Again this type of complex consent was never required by the university's review committees.

Another change was in purchasing. In the first decade of running my lab I could get bids and pick the lowest offer with the best equipment. Later, the university took it out of my hands and got the bids, but often they did not know how to get the best deal and the best equipment. To make matters worse they interfered with how I hired clerical and research assistants. In the early years, I would write a job description and some university committee would go over it for clarity, post it, and send me all the applications. I could choose which applicants to interview. Then they took it out of my hands. They would send me a panel of five to seven people, balanced for race and sex, and I had to give them acceptable reasons for rejecting those people before I could see another group. I no longer could choose whom I wanted to interview.

The straw that broke this camel's back was the requirement to take an online course on sexual harassment. I had never been so charged and regarded the course as a waste of my time. I did it, but when they told me six months later I had to do it again and would have to take such an online course every six months indefinitely, I refused. I knew that such repeated wastes of time were required by the federal government, but I thought the university should protest this waste of the taxpayer's money rather than acquiesce.

If I persisted in my refusal I would not be allowed to submit another research grant. I replied that I would work on other people's grants. That, too, would not be allowed. I decided the time had come to go.

Another contributing factor was that my wife, Mary Ann Mason, had accepted the position as dean of graduate studies at UC Berkeley, a nine-to-five job. We had agreed when we married to move back and forth across the bay, as she loved and worked in the East Bay, and I loved and worked in the city. We had moved twice. Now she required I move to the East Bay, which I did, but the commute going with the traffic over the bay bridge was horrendous. When I told the chairman of psychiatry of my plan to resign, he asked me to reconsider. It was fine, he said, to just come in once a week. I couldn't run a lab that way, and as I have explained, there were other reasons it was no longer reasonable to do research within the university. I planned to retire when I was sixty-five, but when I met the Dalai Lama I took on new responsibilities that led me to postpone retirement until my seventieth birthday in 2004.

I gave a farewell speech to the department of psychiatry where I had spent nearly my entire career (except for the two army years), starting in 1957. I reviewed what I considered to be my major research accomplishments, all of which have been described here. I also outlined what I intended to do in retirement. I was going to learn to play the harmonica, which I had to date only toyed around with, acquiring through gifts from friends, a large collection of superb harmonicas.

I also intended to take photographs of friends I had known for fifty years or more. Typically, portrait photographers are unacquainted with their subjects, producing a likeness but no inkling of the underlying person's character. I had some ideas about how I might capture how my subjects felt about the life they had lived and how I would compare that to how I saw them. I only made two such portraits, in which I accomplished my goal, before I got distracted by my obligations to the Dalai Lama and my decision to translate my research findings into tools people could use to improve their lives.

Just before I retired I wrote my fourteenth book, *Emotions Revealed*, in which I tried to distill just what I thought would be useful for people to know in order to improve their emotional life. Published in 2003, with a second edition in 2009 adding a new chapter on deception, the book remains in print and occasionally is seen in bookstores. I have strong affection for that book. It is the second one I wrote for a general and not an academic audience (the earlier one was *Unmasking the Face* in 1975).

Emotions Revealed contains my theory of emotion as well as hundreds of photographs illustrating how emotion is registered in the face. Academic psychologists have rarely paid it any attention for three reasons: it is not a book reporting data, but theory; it is written in an easy-to-understand fashion; and it has photographs.

CHAPTER 23

Micros and Starting a Startup

IN THE LATE 1960S we discovered micro facial expressions when examining our films of psychiatric patients who had lied during a clinical interview, concealing either plans to commit suicide or hallucinations. We defined micro expressions as being "…so brief that they are barely perceptible to the untrained observer. Micro displays may be fragments of a squelched, neutralized, or masked display. Micro displays may also show the full-muscular movements associated with macro affect display, but may be greatly reduced in time. We have found that such micro displays when shown in slow motion do convey emotional information to observers, and that expert clinical observers can see micro displays and read the emotional information without the benefit of slow motion projection" (p.27).[37]

In our first paper on deception we proposed that "… the face is equipped to lie the most and leak the most, and thus can be a very confusing source of information during deception.... [A person] can get away with and best perpetrate deception through his face. Although he must monitor quickly and work continually to inhibit this fast responsive system, he has most awareness of his facial display and is usually well practiced in the display rules for modulating facial affects.... [T]he face is the major site for lies of commission [through macro expressions, which are large in scope and of sufficient duration to be readily seen].... [Most people will ignore or disregard such] important sources of information as micro displays and the rough edges on the simulated display.... One would expect the usual observer of the face typically to be misled. One would expect the keen observer, on the other hand, to receive contradictory information from facial cues: simulated messages, micro leakage of information which contradicts the simulations, and deception clues of squelched displays and improperly performed simulations" (pp. 98–99)." [38]

By this reasoning people who are highly trained in observing facial movement might have made accurate judgments when they saw the videotapes of the subjects who had lied or told the truth about the emotions they felt. We showed the face-only videotapes to four associates who had been using our first technique for measuring the face[39] for more than a year. Each of these four people achieved an accuracy score of 80 percent or higher. So the face does contain accurate information, as well as misinformation, when people lie. Most people respond to the macro expressions and are misled, while a few keen observers detect the micro expressions and other imperfections in the macro displays and are correctly informed.

Many of the signs of lying that we have identified are not shown by everyone. Their absence does not mean a person is truthful, but their presence, especially when there are multiple different types of signs (e.g., a fragment of a shrug and micro expressions), is very suggestive. Thus, it appears that while most people are not attuned to the recognition of micro expressions, most can learn to become sensitive to them. We do not know how long improvement gained through training is maintained.

In situations in which distinguishing lies from truthful statements is the focus, great care must be taken not to make either of two mistakes. First, the absence of micro expressions, like the absence of gestural slips, does not prove a person is truthful; not all liars show such signs.

The second mistake is to presume that concealed emotion is evidence that a person is lying about the topic of interest to the interviewer. We need to be careful to avoid what I have called Othello's error. He mistakenly assumed that Desdemona's expression of fear was the reaction of a woman caught in betrayal. He failed to understand that emotions do not tell you their cause.

The fear of being disbelieved looks the same as the fear of being caught. In real-life lies that I have studied people suspected of crimes sometimes show micro expressions of anger. Only through further questioning is it possible to determine whether the concealed anger is the result of being wrongfully under suspicion or whether it is anger toward the interviewer for trying to catch the suspect in a misdeed. Lying about the topic of interest should be the last, not the first, explanation of why a micro expression has occurred.

Micros can occur for two very different reasons: deliberate suppression or unconscious repression. The resulting micro looked the same, so what caused the micro would have to be deduced from either the circumstances in which they occur or questioning.

The people I taught how to recognize micros loved it, even cops, who started out doubtful a professor could teach them anything useful. In the words of one L.A. policeman who spoke at a public event in my honor, "his shit works!" But it was very dull to teach. I began to explore how I could make a training tool, first on a DVD and later online, so I would not have to teach it. After many mistakes, I had a DVD I could sell on the Internet, and with the income from those sales I formed the Paul Ekman Group (PEG) to develop and market online training tools based on my research. METT Intensive, the Micro Expressions Intensive Training Tool, takes about forty minutes to complete. There is a benchmark, in which you try to spot the emotion in very quickly flashed expressions. Then comes a training segment in which morphed images contrast the ways in which emotions appear on the face in slow motion. A practice session gives feedback after each judgment, with some voice-over commentaries about what to look for. A review, and then the Improvement Measure, in which new expressions much like the ones that appeared in the benchmark section appear.

On average most people obtain 30 to 40 percent accuracy in the benchmark, and move up to 70 to 80 percent in the Improvement Measure. I make METT Intensive available without cost to anyone doing research, and now there is evidence from other scientists that METT

Intensive improves the ability of schizophrenics to spot emotion, benefits sales persons, and aids in detecting lies. Many people are now trying it with autism and Asperger's.

The income from METT Intensive allowed me to add a full-time assistant to PEG and build SETT, the Subtle Emotion Training Tool. These are very small expressions in just one region of the face. They may be the first sign of an emotion that is just beginning, or leakage of a strongly felt emotion. SETT also takes less than an hour, and others have found it helps in detecting lies. Over the years I made improvements and added features, but now METT Intensive and SETT are completed. Without advertising or sales personnel we have sold one-third of a million copies, which pays for my staff of four, office space, etc. The Defense Department told me that they wanted a version that would get most people to 95 to 100 percent recognition. I built METT Intensive, which takes nearly three hours to complete. The last tool in what I call the *face suite* focuses on recognizing micro expressions from a profile view, not full face. It is different but learnable.

When METT Intensive first was offered for sale online, I blocked anyone using a credit card from a nondemocratic country. My friends in the Defense Department told me not to do so. The governments had workarounds, and all I was blocking was the civilian populations in those countries. So I opened it up, hoping it is doing more good than harm for people to better know how others are feeling, even when people are trying to conceal their emotions.

I developed another online training tool—Responding Effectively Training Tool, or RETT for short. It helps you to consider how to best respond to another person's emotions in a difficult situation. For example, your spouse is out of town, you are having dinner with your new boss, and the babysitter just called, saying she has the flu. You tell your adolescent offspring that he or she can't go out bowling with friends as planned, but has to babysit the younger sister. The adolescent says, "thanks for telling me" but in one take the adolescent shows sadness in face and voice, and in another take anger is shown. When each emotion is shown, a list of six or seven responses the parent might then make is displayed. The user picks the best one, and I pop up giving feedback about the pros and cons of that choice, asking the user to pick another response, giving feedback, and so on.

Before the user starts, they select whether there has been a close or strained relationship between parent and offspring. Whichever the user selects, after completing all the parts, after all the responses and all the feedback, they are asked to do it again, but this time choosing a different relationship between parent and offspring. It takes about an hour, but doesn't have to be done in one sitting. All that I am describing is shown in broadcast-quality video, not questionnaires.

In addition to the family scenario that I have described, we have a work scenario and a criminal justice scenario. I recruited experts in family relationships, in the workplace, and criminal justice to help me create RETT.

The purpose of RETT is to encourage the user to consider how to respond to another person's emotions—to realize that there are choices, some more helpful than others.

The last of my online training tools is a few months from completion. It is a tool for couples to explore how they view each other, using graphics, not questionnaires. The output allows a couple to see the differences in how each person experiences an emotion such as anger, and whether each person's view of him- or herself is shared by the partner's view of him or her. It is very interesting, engaging, and sometimes shocking to see.

Creating these tools is a lot of work, takes a lot of money and a lot of time, and although I have thought of other training tools, I am resisting making any more. I would prefer to put my time into writing more books and blogs, which costs a lot less and is a more solitary activity. But I have come to know that I am a very poor predictor of what I am going to do next. The next major adventure in my life, a life-changer, is a good example of that.

CHAPTER 24

Becoming Close Friends with the Dalai Lama, 2000–2015

I WAS PROUD of not having been seduced by any of the intellectual-spiritual fads that swept through San Francisco. I avoided Transactional Analysis, Synanon, Erhard Seminar Training (EST), and a few others whose names I can no longer recall. The one current in the 1990s was Buddhism, mindfulness, and the Dalai Lama. I would have ignored it too but my fifteen-year-old daughter had gotten interested in the plight of the Tibetan people. A teacher from her private high school had taken a group of kids trekking in Nepal for five weeks. We didn't know that in the last week each kid would live with a Tibetan family in a refugee camp in Katmandu.

Eve, a natural activist, became a strong advocate for Free Tibet, forming the largest high school Free Tibet club in America, leafleting and organizing boycotts of companies that did not hire Tibetans in Tibet, but instead employed Han Chinese recent immigrants. She was invited with a half dozen other kids her age to meet the Dalai Lama, and was moved.

Some of my academic psychology colleagues, I learned, had been interested in Buddhist contemplative practices for a long time. I had heard through them that the Dalai Lama was very interested in science, holding weeklong meetings at which he invited a handful of scientists to discuss issues of interest to him. If you were invited you were able to bring a silent observer for the week. What a treat I thought that would be for Eve, and for that reason I put my name in for the next meeting, to be chaired by Daniel Goleman, on Destructive Emotions.

It was the practice of Mind and Life, the organization that arranged these meetings, to hold a pre-meeting at which each of the invitees would give a summary of what they planned to present and get feedback on how it might be understood by the Dalai Lama. I presented my rather hard-nosed, no holds barred, empirical approach. "If you can't measure it, better to put off considering it until it became possible to measure it," was my philosophy. I remember hearing that many of the participants who attended, and in particular Alan Wallace, a renowned Buddhist scholar, thought I would be a bad fit, and wished they could take back the invitation. Dan Goleman, who was to chair the meeting with the Dalai, recently wrote this account:

> *When Richard Davidson and I were considering which scientists to invite to participate in the Mind and Life meeting on "Destructive Emotions," we had misgivings about*

Paul, despite his being at the top of our list. Our hesitation had to do with Paul's tough-mindedness as a scientist—we were unsure what his chemistry might be with the Dalai Lama—and we know that beyond first-class science, personal rapport made these meetings work. And, as Paul has said himself, at first during the meeting he had his own doubts.

I am not surprised by their doubts, for I was going there solely to give my daughter an opportunity to be in the same room with the Dalai Lama for five days, not because of any interest myself in him or Buddhist thinking.

It was not an easy matter to get to Dharamsala, where the meetings were held in his palace in exile. Also in the group were the late Francesco Varela, a Chilean neuroscientist who had first organized these meetings, some years earlier founding an organization named "Mind and Life" for this purpose; my friend and collaborator neuropsychologist Richie Davidson; the French monk Matthieu Ricard; the developmental psychologist Mark Greenberg; the cultural psychologist Jeanne Tsai (a former student of mine); and the philosopher Owen Flanagan. I introduced Eve to the Dalai Lama as my spiritual leader, telling him, without explaining it, that she was the reason I was there. In retrospect, I think that was a mistake, but it ended up not mattering. But let me not get ahead of the story, for this meeting was to change my life forever. That didn't happen until the third day.

The palace grounds were beautiful, as was the meeting room, and the Dalai Lama was in the most modest fashion imaginable, awe-inspiring. Something I was to get to know much better, but still do not understand. Matthieu Ricard, the former biologist, now a monk for more than thirty years, who was to become one of my closest friends, spoke first, explaining to the scientists the principal tenets of Buddhism. The second day of the meeting was to be mine, explaining a Darwinian view of emotion in the morning, with discussion of my presentation by the Dalai Lama and the group in the afternoon.

I was disappointed that the only part of my presentation that the Dalai Lama asked about was my distinction between moods and emotions. I thought this was the least important of what I presented, but the Dalai Lama was not familiar with this distinction, and it not only made sense to him, but helped him understand himself. Briefly, what I said about moods was that they not only last longer than emotions, but they are saturated with a particular emotion: anger in an irritable mood; sadness in a blue mood; fear in a worried mood; and enjoyment in a high mood. Unlike emotions, we often don't know what triggered a mood, but recognizing what mood we are in can be helpful as a caution, for we are likely to over-react emotionally when we are in the grip of a mood.

When the morning session was over, I was disappointed that the Dalai Lama had made so few comments. I had not yet learned how to tell when he is paying attention or is bored (when interested, he leans forward in his chair; leaning back occurs when he is bored, disinterested, or tired). I had hopes that the afternoon session would provoke discussion, but Dan Goleman, who chaired the discussion, allowed it to drift into matters totally unrelated to my talk.

At the end of the day I told Anne Harrington (a history professor at Harvard who was monitoring the meetings and interviewing the participants) it had been a waste of my time and the Dalai Lama's time. I was thoroughly disenchanted. There was one exception. Buddhist scholar Alan Wallace was excited by my idea of a refractory period, which typically occurs when an emotion is first experienced, filtering the information available to the person experiencing an emotion. Only information that sustains the emotion gets through, or is available from memory. The refractory period focuses attention and can be useful in the first moments, but problematic if it continues for long. Alan said this concept offered a useful bridge to key Buddhist thinking about attention and awareness. Only now do I understand why Alan's complex accounts of attention might utilize my concept of a refractory period. I remember Dan criticizing my choice of words, since a refractory period has been used to describe the period following sexual intercourse before another episode of sexual arousal and performance can be accomplished. I still use the phrase refractory period in my writing.

I cannot remember who spoke on the third day. I think it was Jeanne Tsai in the morning who talked about her research on cultural differences in emotion. The Dalai Lama made clear he was not interested in differences, but in universals. Jeanne was very disappointed in his reaction. Mark Greenberg, a developmental psychologist, described his very interesting work with children.

There were breaks every few hours when participants and the silent observers went outside, had a cup of tea, and stretched. The Dalai Lama did not leave the room but made clear this was a time when observers could talk to him individually. Tuesday night, Eve had told me she wanted to ask him how a celibate monk could understand love. She didn't ask that impertinent question, but instead she asked why we get the angriest at those we love. It is a good question, and a less aggressive one as well.

I am quoting now from the last chapter of my publication of the dialogue with the Dalai Lama, *Emotional Awareness*. The last chapter focuses on the life-changing experience, which I could not explain.

Ekman: Sometimes, for seemingly inexplicable reasons, and without seeking or expecting it, a major change occurs in how one experiences life. For me, when such a change occurred around the turn of the millennium, its impact was startling and perplexing because none of the tools I had spent a lifetime perfecting as a research psychologist equipped me to make sense of what had happened. Given the mysterious nature of my change, I would have dismissed it except that the benefits were quite great, not just to me but to those who dealt with me on a daily basis.

The change in my life was a dramatic shift in how I experienced emotion—my very own professional bailiwick. It occurred during our first meeting in Dharamsala, India, in 2000. [Reader, remember I am quoting from an actual dialogue with the Dalai Lama that was published in 2008.] It was a riddle. As a scientist, I was used to seeking explanations but also comfortable when some things could not yet be explained, which was one of the reasons I had never been drawn to any religion, let alone Buddhism, which I didn't yet know was not like any of the Abrahamic religions. There is no dogma, no word from God.

Overly intense anger had been a plague in my life until then: It began shortly after the last time my father hit me, when I was eighteen. I warned him that if he hit me again, I would hit him back. He regarded this as a threat and called the police to arrest me for threatening his life. I had to flee my home forever. Since then, very few days would go by without my having an angry impulse on which I would act in a way that I regretted afterward (although I never hit anyone). I was constantly on guard, trying not to yield to such impulses and often failing. I do not think a week of my life went by, from the time I was eighteen until the time I was sixty-six [in 2000] that I did not have a couple of regrettable episodes of anger. Not a wonderful way to lead your life.

Then, for seven months, not one angry impulse. Not one. I was freed; it was a wonderful relief. I asked Alan Wallace, "What's happening?" and he said that this was "not at all unusual—but expect it to fade over time."

He was right. It did fade over time, but never back to where it had been. I do have angry impulses, and I do sometimes act on them, but not all the time. Sometimes I recognize the impulse and just let it pass by me, even when provoked. I am not able to do this all the time, but my experience of anger is very different than before. The chief exceptions are when I am very tired, having not had enough sleep, or when I am experiencing physical pain due to some medical problem. Even then, my anger is not as severe as it typically was before my visit to D'sala.

During that meeting in D'sala, you [I am here referring to the Dalai Lama to whom I am speaking] did not get up during the breaks. Everyone else got up, stretched, and drank some tea. You remained seated so that the observers could come up and talk to you for a few minutes. My daughter, Eve, wanted to ask you a question.

During one break, Eve and I sat down on either side of you, and I told you in just a few words about her. She asked and you answered her question: "Why do we get the angriest at those we are in love with?" Your reply suggested it was because they fail to meet our unrealistic, idealized expectations of them. Focus on and accept their flaws and you will not be disappointed, and that source of anger will fade. You and she talked for about eight minutes.

During this whole time, you held my hand in one of your hands. I never said another word after introducing Eve, but I had two unusual experiences. One was that I had a very strong physical sensation for which I do not have an English word—it comes closest to "warmth," but there was no heat. It certainly felt very good, and like nothing I have felt before or after. The other experience was that looking out into the large room was like looking at the world through the wrong side of the binoculars. Although people were quite close, maybe four feet away, so they could watch what was happening, it appeared to me as if they were hundreds of feet away.

Dalai Lama: Sometimes you actually experience that kind of vision—distant vision.

Ekman: It was as if the three of us were encapsulated, tightly bound, and everyone else was off in the distance. I told a number of people about this experience and asked them if they knew of anyone else who shared it. I asked Thupten Jinpa [a longtime translator and expert on the Buddhist classics], Alan Wallace [a former monk and Buddhist scholar], and Matthieu Ricard [an author, and a monk for more than thirty years]. They were all familiar with what I described, each of them saying they had witnessed it many times. They gave me the names of other people they had observed having the same experience.

I interviewed eight of these people. None of the other eight had their child with them, so that cannot be necessary. They all described a transformation of their lives, a change in the direction of their lives, and a change in their emotional lives; that was common. They were also all at a transition point in their lives. One or two had just recovered from a life-threatening illness; another had just had a divorce; another was just about to change jobs. It was a transition point for me also: I had made the decision to retire from the university, which I subsequently postponed for four years, so that I could organize research that you asked be initiated at the meeting.

I think many Americans lead their lives in such a way that they cannot see anything on either side of them. It is as if they are in the Olympic event called the Luge, in which there are high walls on either side. You are moving very fast; if you look to the left or the right, you might crash. You just speed ahead as fast as you can. That is how I was leading my life, how most scientists I know lead their lives. They never see alternative paths in life once they start on the race to discover. But each of these eight people were at a transition point, able to look to the left and to the right, to see alternative paths in life.

And one more characteristic—they each had a severe emotional wound in their lives that had never healed. They reported that after their meeting with you, the wound did not disappear, but was enormously improved.

I remain a skeptic about how to explain what happened, but I am convinced a major reorganization in my emotional life occurred. I am a little worried that many Western scientists might think I have gone nuts, especially when they read what I am now going to tell you about what it felt like. *(Dalai Lama and Jinpa laugh.)*

What I was experiencing was an intense, very unusual feeling, which felt very good; it felt as if it was radiating. The other eight people I interviewed also used the term "radiate" when describing their experiences.

I have given you my first-person, phenomenological description. As a scientist, I do not know how to explain it, but that does not mean it is not susceptible to scientific explanation; I just do not know where to start, and I suspect we do not yet have the proper tools to examine this phenomenon objectively.

The change that occurred in me was very dramatic. When I left D'sala, I met my wife in New Delhi, so that we could spend two weeks traveling in India. My wife said, "You are not the man I married."

Dalai Lama: Really?

Ekman: She said, "I had not asked for a change." Then, the next day, she said, "Oh, I am so glad. You are so much easier to be with," and she still says this. In fact, I talked to her last night, and she again said, "Be sure to thank His Holiness, because the last seven years have been our happiest."

I now believe that this experience was involved in the end of my hatred; the platform for my too-ready anger was no longer in place, and so the anger itself receded. In the last seven years there have been maybe two incidents where I would say I could have handled anger better. Now most of the time, when my wife gets angry at me, I do not get angry. Most of the time—this is the funny part—I avoid it. I say, "I can see you are angry. Let us talk about it when you are not angry. I do not want to talk now because your anger might get me angry. I do not want to get angry." *(Dalai Lama chuckles.)*

I used to think, I am being a coward. Now I am going to say to her, "I am being a Buddhist. I am going to avoid dealing with your anger now. We will talk about it when you are over the anger." Angry people do not like that. They want to fight.

Dalai Lama: Yes. That is right.

Ekman: Why did these changes occur in my life? Why did they happen to the other people I interviewed? Some people who have heard my account have said, "Oh, it is because you look up to the Dalai Lama so much." It is not true. I had zero knowledge of Buddhism when we first met in 2000 when this happened. I thought you were, from what I read, an advocate of non-violence, like Gandhi, and I respected that, but I had little sympathy with Buddhism.

It was not because I was expecting a miracle. I do not believe miracles occur; that is religious, and I am not religious. How do you explain it?

Dalai Lama: Of course, from the Buddhist viewpoint, I do not know. From common sense . . . I do not know. I think your base nature [is] a pleasant nature, I think, more honest, and [a person] who recognizes what is positive—I think that is the main factor. The very nature of our discussions also; they are dealing with emotions, and these things, and automatically [focus on] the value of compassion and the recognition of the destructiveness of anger or hatred. So that also is one factor. Then, [by] my side, of course, [it is] not only me; I think the whole atmosphere also makes the difference; and all the other persons generally make for a more calm mind. Anyway, I think the secular—regarding simpler principles—most of our talk has been more spiritual-minded.

Not necessarily *religious* faith, but awareness about the values. From [a] Buddhist viewpoint, of course, the karmic factor is also there. Whether you are from a Buddhist viewpoint, or whether you accept or not, or whether you know or not that there is limitless life, there is some acquaintance; that is also there. I do not know. So, now [what is] important is [finding] satisfaction. Some benefit there, some positive things there: that is enough. *(Laughs)* I am not to say, to find [the] answer [of] how it happened, why it happened, or how it happened, in this case.

Ekman: As a scientist, I cannot ignore what I experienced. It is not that I had not earlier tried other approaches to ameliorate my problems with anger. Three times in my life I was a patient in psychoanalysis, in part to try to deal with this terrible problem of anger. Yet, no change. I think the change that occurred within me started with that physical sensation, whatever it was. I think that what I experienced was—a non-scientific term—*goodness*. Every one of the other eight people I interviewed said they felt goodness; they felt it radiating and felt the same kind of warmth that I did. I have no idea what it is or how it happens, but it is not in my imagination. Though we do not have the tools to understand it, that does not mean it does not exist.

I have to mention another thing, which is that during our first meeting in Dharamsala, I had this feeling—in the West, we call it déjà vu—as if I had known you all my life.

Dalai Lama: That is right, that is right.

Ekman: The only people who can explain this that I know of are Buddhists: that I would have known you in some previous life. That is not part of my belief, yet I do feel as if I have known you all of my life!

Dalai Lama: That is, I think, a very clear sign, some kind of imprint, I think, from the past. So that means within this lifetime, you see, no, it did not happen. So, that means some previous life.

Ekman: The experience is closest to how I feel towards my sister and my aunt. I have known them since I was born. I have not known you since I was born, but it is as if—

Dalai Lama: And also the attitude, I think, [of] being a scientist, thinking more widely, more open. That also [makes] a difference. It is a kind of mystery, actually. One of the characteristics of mysteries, of anything that is a mystery, is that it is not untrue—it is a fact. Yet its underlying conditions and explanations are opaque and hidden to us. Maybe scientists would not have much to say about this phenomenon; it is not connected to science; it is not your business. *(Several people laugh, including the Dalai Lama.)* Something happened—okay. It is positive; it is good. So from the Buddhist viewpoint, the karmic link, not only in this life but also in previous times or in past lives, that is also a factor.

One of the key inspirational prayers that Buddhists make on a daily basis is: "May anyone who comes into contact with me, whether they hear about me or they see me or they think about me, experience a benefit and happiness." That is an important part of the daily prayer. Maybe there is some effect of this kind of prayer on people who do it continually, on a daily basis. But then, of course, among the Tibetans there are hundreds and thousands who do these kinds of prayers on a daily basis!

Ekman: I agree with you that if it is a mystery that does not mean it is not a fact. And I agree with you that just because science at this time cannot explain something does not mean that we should not try to do so. I suspect that there is something about contemplative practice that generates, in some people, a small number of people, a *goodness*—I cannot think of another word, though this is not a twenty-first century word—but a kind of goodness that is of benefit to others. Historically, there have been accounts of such experiences.

There are many mysteries still. Some people think that if it is a mystery, it cannot be ever illuminated, but that is not my view. It is a mystery, but I do not know whether it will always be a mystery or whether someday we will be able to understand it. It would be nice to better understand this experience, which had such benefit, so that we could provide a similar benefit to other people.

Dalai Lama: This is not exactly at the level of mystery that we were talking about, but it is kind of—semi-mystery *(laughing)*. As a result of my dialogues with scientists, I am questioning many of the descriptions and assumptions of Buddhist cosmology. Some could say I have become a heretic!

Ekman: It is such a difficult thing to do—to examine, over time, the sequence of what occurs. Yet, it seems to me that people such as you and Matthieu Ricard are uniquely able to do this. We can learn from that because you are what Varela talked about: highly skilled observers of your own mental processes.

Most of us are not such highly skilled observers of our inner thoughts and feelings. The issue, of course, is for us to learn some of those skills from those who are highly skilled, to be able to learn how to develop the skills, and become more observant of the sequence of our subjective experiences.

Dalai Lama: Part of the monastic educational training is debate-oriented, always looking for inconsistencies and posing critical questions. Thus some of the Western teachers who have taught science in the monasteries have said they enjoyed teaching the monks very much because they are always asking critical questions, challenging and stimulating each other. Maybe it is that monastic debate background that makes a difference.

Tibetans have inherited an intellectual culture from the great Indian masters of Nala University, who have provided us with avenues of critical reasoning and methods of analysis. But we should not confine the scope of our analysis simply to the fields that we have been familiar with for thousands of years. We now need to somehow expand this scope, and continue to use the same analysis in other areas.

Jinpa: And in the monastic debate culture, often one of the—

Dalai Lama: Drawbacks.

Jinpa:—is that it tends to rely heavily on citations from authoritative texts. His Holiness has expressed the hope that one day, a new—

Dalai Lama: Now!

Jinpa: From now on, we should modify the system, so that we do not rely on any statements from the authoritative texts but rather more on the reasoning, the path of reasoning.

Dalai Lama: I found a statement made by one of Francisco Varela's teachers very helpful. The teacher said that as scientists we should not become attached to our research. I often tell my fellow Buddhist colleagues that as Buddhists we should ensure that we do not become attached to Buddhism. *(Breaks into laughter.)*

End of selection from my dialogue with the Dalai Lama.

I am sorry to say that I still am not able to figure out what occurred to produce those changes in my emotional life. I have just accepted that they are there, that I still get angry at times, but it is nowhere near the problem it once was in my life. Chief exception is when I feel pain continuously; it has the same influence as being in an irritable mood: I am ready to become angry and get angry easily, so I must work hard to guard against anger running my life once again.

In this meeting in 2000 on the fourth day, after I had this mysterious experience and was feeling transformed in ways I could not understand, the Dalai Lama asked in the morning session if this was just going to be good talk, good Karma, or was something going to happen because of our discussions. He was looking directly at me when he said that, a fact I confirmed when I later inspected the video that had been recorded of the meetings.

I was surprised to hear myself say that I was no longer a pessimist, and as a newly minted optimist I thought something could be done, if we were to combine Western approaches to developing emotional skills with Buddhist practices to increase momentary awareness. If the governor of California was to say that he wanted us to increase the emotional awareness and empathy of prison guards, how many hours did the Dalai Lama think it would take to make a noticeable difference? Without a moment's pause he said forty-eight hours. I said I would, with the help of those present, undertake the organization of a course that came to be known as Cultivating Emotional Balance (CEB). The Dalai urged that the training be secular, not Buddhist, in theoretical orientation.

I was very impressed with Alan Wallace, and am to this day impressed by his brilliance, dedication, and talents as a teacher. The Dalai Lama seemed to have confidence in Alan, and had been one of his main teachers and guides when Alan was a Buddhist monk for eight years. I did not know enough then to know what a mistake I was making in asking Alan to be responsible for the contemplative side of CEB, for Alan cannot teach without incorporating Buddhist theory and concepts very explicitly.

With input from Mark Greenberg and Richie Davidson, I developed the outlines of the Western part of the emotional skills training in CEB. At a meeting a year later in Madison, Wisconsin, I reported that CEB was ready to go, the planning was done, all we needed was the money to do it. It would be costly because we were committed to doing a careful before-after evaluation of whether CEB was of benefit. The Dalai Lama surprised me by asking how much it would cost, and even more when he heard my estimate of $600,000 that he would give us the first $50,000. It nearly knocked me off my chair.

Fortunately the cameras were recording the meeting when the Dalai Lama made this offer, and with some help I had that portion of the video made into a short fund-raiser, in which John Cleese (whom I had gotten to know when I consulted on a film he made for the BBC on the face) did the narration. With that fund-raising film and the help of Jon Kabat-Zinn and Dan Goleman I raised $800,000 in a few months. I trained a local psychologist, Margaret Cullen, who was a certified trainer of Jon Kabat-Zinn's approach to contemplative practice, in how to teach the emotional skills part that I created.

True to the Dalai Lama's suggestion the training was about forty-eight hours, with weekly meetings of three hours, a weekend retreat, and another weekend day. Alan provided the contemplative training, and I observed, with Margaret Kemeny, a psychologist on the faculty at UCSF and an expert in evaluating clinical trials, to oversee the research evaluation of the benefits of CEB. We selected four training schoolteachers in the San Francisco school system who had no previous relevant training, but who we expected would likely be under some stress from their demanding, under-supported, and underpaid jobs.

Watching CEB, I was very impressed with what I saw and I was confident the measures would show a benefit. About this time, I was afflicted with a series of abdominal surgeries, and had to turn over the entire CEB evaluation to Margaret Kemeny, who carried it through. Even if illness had not impaired me, I would have sought out Margaret to do the evaluation of CEB, for this type of research is her bailiwick, not mine. Unfortunately it took her decades to complete the analysis and get an article published.[40] If she had been prompt, it would have been one of the first studies to show very large benefits from combining Western and Eastern approaches to emotion; instead it was one of many. It did show major benefits on measures of stress, anxiety, and depression, as large as any reported for any other intervention.

I was scheduled to teach CEB with Alan at a meditation center in Thailand, with my daughter, Eve, as my assistant. But I was laid low by illness, and Eve did the teaching with my participation remotely by Skype. Eve, with Alan Wallace, has now trained, in five weeklong sessions, more than two hundred people to teach CEB. Eve herself continues to also teach CEB directly. CEB lives on.

In 2004 I saw an advertisement for a public meeting in Vancouver entitled "Balancing Educating the Mind with Educating the Heart." Eve and I flew up to Vancouver to attend the meeting. On the stage, a distinguished group answered the question of what had opened their heart. Professor Jo-Ann Archibald (UBC) said it was her Canadian native people's religion. Rabbi Zalman Schachter said it was his faith in Judaism. Bishop Tutu said it was Christianity. And the honorable Shirin Ebadi said it was her belief in Islam. Last to speak was the Dalai Lama, who after chuckling when he looked at each one of them, said something to the effect "don't you know that differences in religious beliefs have been the source of most of the wars? We should focus instead on what unites us, which are our emotions."

I was pleased and worried—pleased that he was using what he had heard me talk about and was making use of it, but worried that he was focusing only on what unites us, not recognizing that our emotions also divide us. By the time I returned to San Francisco I had developed a list of thirty issues about the nature of emotion that I thought I should try to discuss with the Dalai Lama, so he would have a more realistic evaluation of what emotions are. I didn't yet know that most Buddhist thinkers regard most emotions as "afflictions," mental states to be avoided or mental states that one has to rise above.

Did I have the right to ask for this leader of the Tibetan people in exile for any of his precious time? I feared being presumptuous, but at the same time I felt a responsibility to enlarge his perspective on emotions. I knew he was very grateful for my evidence on universals, for anything which unites us is important to his thinking, but I also knew he was a thinker who enjoyed complexities and he didn't have it about my topic, emotion.

I sent my list of thirty issues that needed to be discussed to Thupten Jinpa and Alan Wallace, asking them if they thought it would be important to discuss them with the Dalai Lama. They both encouraged me, and Jinpa brought my list to the Dalai Lama's attention. I heard back from Tenzin Taklha, his most senior and, I have come to think, influential of the people who manage the Dalai Lama's schedule, that I would be invited to meet with the Dalai Lama as soon as time in his very busy schedule became available.

A few months later I was told that I could meet with the Dalai Lama for up to twelve hours, spread over four days, at the Pritzker family farm outside of Chicago. I later learned that his evaluation at the Mayo Clinic (which he has yearly) had taken less time than anticipated. There was a gap of four days before his next commitment, which could not be moved up.

I brought with me my wife, Mary Ann, my daughter, Eve, and my stepson Tom, to be silent observers. I also invited Clifford Saron to obtain a high-quality audio recording of our discussions, just in case there might be further use of my discussion with the Dalai Lama. Cliff is a very techy perfectionist; actually he is also a perfectionist about everything scientific, a very serious scientist who was soon to lead the most intensive and extensive study ever done on the impact of contemplative practices on the mind. I knew Jinpa would be there as both translator and consultant on complex Buddhist issues, for Jinpa has been translating classic Buddhist texts for many years.

I never met the Pritzkers, who were living there. I was told she was working for a Ph.D. in Judaic studies at the University of Chicago. Reportedly the farm housed a superb collection of Himalayan art. Our group waited for the meeting to begin in a small separate building with a Tibetan woman who spoke no English. We were told she had just been released from a Chinese jail, where she had spent more than a decade for the criminal offense of having a picture of the Dalai Lama in her purse. She was waiting to meet the Dalai Lama, before being taken elsewhere to live in the United States.

The U.S. State department provides protective security for heads of state and other senior foreign officials. Round the clock there was a group of them taking turns. In front of the farmhouse, a large SUV was parked with the engine always running, in case there should be a need for a fast departure. The Dalai Lama's own protective security people were there as well.

After an hour's wait we were ushered into the large room where our meeting occurred. I sat close to the Dalai Lama, at a right angle to his chair. Before we began I was struggling with the fear that after an hour, he would dismiss me, thanking me very much for coming. What an embarrassing disappointment that would be! I don't think most people know that my initial expectations always involve rejection, an unwanted but pervasive inheritance, still alive in my mind.

That didn't happen. Instead we had a vigorous discussion. I later learned that the Dalai Lama loves to argue, had received more training in debating than in contemplative practices, and relished the opportunity for vigorous argument. Which is what we had. I began to explain the first on my list of issues, but I didn't get very far before we were going back and forth, exchanging ideas about what I had raised, disagreeing with each other, exchanging sides in the friendliest and most passionate discussion of ideas I have ever had. I loved it. So, apparently, did he.

I was to tell him in a later meeting how much I enjoyed our vigorous intellectual arguments. I didn't have to be afraid of anger arising as part of the arguments. We were both immensely curious as to where our debating would lead. There was a great deal of passion with no rancor, no personal stake in who was right; often we were both wrong. He very often found a way to introduce a joke, relevant to what we were discussing, but resulting in peals of laughter. We had a great time.

At the end of three hours, he put his shoes back on, unfolded his legs from a lotus position, signaling the end of our meeting. He warmly said he looked forward to our next meeting tomorrow. What a joy; what a relief; what fun. We were staying at a nearby motel, and I can't remember anything else about the rest of the day and evening.

My mind was focused then, as it is now, on our joyous, vigorous discussion.

At the end of the four days, after twelve hours of the most intellectual fun I had ever had, we were only halfway through my list. He wanted to continue, inviting me to come to D'Sala to continue our discussion as soon as I could. I went there twice more, again audio recording our exchanges. After nearly forty hours of recorded discussions, we had come to common ground on many issues, issues I had not previously explored in depth, for never before, or after, have I ever spent so much time discussing these matters with anyone, let alone such a bright, funny person.

Everything I take for granted, without realizing it, he does not. Everything he takes for granted, I do not. Our discussions exposed for scrutiny these implicit assumptions about not just the nature of emotion, but what life is about, for both of us think that emotions are at the center of life.

I let Tenzin Taklha know that I had edited our discussions, not cutting anything but collecting together discussions held at different meetings about the same topic. I was ready to submit it to a publisher. I was asked to come to D'Sala again. The Dalai Lama asked me how the authorship would be listed. I was charmed by the fact that he, like me, would be concerned about how credit is shared. He is not a saint: he still struggles with anger, and he still sometimes acts in a way he later regrets (but rarely). I told him that since D comes before E, the authorship would be Dalai Lama and Paul Ekman. He was pleased. I asked him if he agreed that I should now seek a publisher. He replied, not before I read the whole book aloud to him.

Tenzin Taklha objected that there was no time in his schedule to do that. The Dalai Lama told him to make time. So I read from what was to become the book *Emotional Awareness* for four hours every day. Of course, the Dalai Lama kept thinking of further matters we needed to discuss, and the book grew by a third. Again, it was great fun, revealing new insights, better understanding of the role of awareness, the key to having choice about whether to engage emotionally. We agreed that nature does not give you that awareness; just the opposite. Emotions save our lives because they apply past learned experience (as well as the wisdom of the ages) to solving immediate problems without thought, immediately. If we are to not respond mistakenly we need to shine the light of awareness on the onset of emotions. What my psychotherapy supervisor Frank Gorman advocated in my last year of clinical training—increase the gap between the impulse and the action so there can be time for consideration—the Buddhists say the same thing, recognize the spark before the flame.

Thinking back, for it has been seven years since those discussions ended, I think there were two major, important new ideas, new for both of us. First, don't regard any emotion as a problem; it depends on how it is experienced. Every emotion can serve us if we can be aware of when we feel that emotion and choose whether and how to engage. Trying to avoid emotions is not possible without leading a life withdrawn from the world. The other idea is that the criterion for a constructive versus destructive enactment of an emotion is whether it furthers or detracts from further collaborations. A simple idea, but it works, and people who learn about it find it useful.

You may have noticed that I have not utilized the honorific title "your holiness" and avoid the abbreviation. Most American scientists use HHDL, which stands for His Holiness the Dalai Lama. That title I believe is totally inappropriate to this man, almost an insult in my mind to call him that. When he first had to go out into the world to represent the Tibetan nation in exile, his advisers chose how the Pope is addressed for his title. I won't do it because the Pope and the Dalai Lama are opposites; the Pope is not to be questioned, he speaks to God. The Buddha said if what I say works for you then use it, but if it doesn't, discard it. How different can they be? Of course, as an agnostic, I don't regard anyone as holy. I think my non-reverential regard for the Dalai Lama is essential to why we get along so well.

Two years ago I was invited by Tenzin Taklha to write something to be given, with the contributions of others, to the Dalai Lama on his seventy-ninth birthday. Here is what I wrote:

Why I don't call the Dalai Lama "Your Holiness"

That is how the pope is addressed, whose statements are not to be questioned for they come to him from God. By contrast the Dalai Lama is eager to modify his beliefs to accommodate scientific findings. He is an explorer of ideas, flexible not dogmatic. (I should also note that I don't regard anyone as holy.)

The Dalai Lama is extraordinary in many ways:

- *I have never met anyone who is having such a good time, continually seeing the humorous side of nearly every situation, without sarcasm or ridicule, never humor that diminishes another person.*

- *The power of his focused attention is astounding.*

- *There is transparency between the public and private Dalai Lama, which is not so for many charismatic leaders whose private lives are distinctly less attractive than their public persona.*

- *He is devoted to compassion, to relieving the suffering of all human beings, what I call stranger compassion.*

- *It feels good to be in his presence. Why? I believe, and I deliberately italicize that word, that he exudes goodness, perhaps not all the time, but much of the time. I suspect the goodness he exudes is related to the compassion he so strongly feels. Alas, science cannot yet study these phenomena.*

The Dalai Lama is a Mozart of the mind, showing what we can aspire towards. It would be just as foolish for us to believe that through practices we can reach his level as to believe music lessons would allow us to become the equal of Mozart. But we can all improve. The Dalai Lama not only illuminates the goal but a path to move towards it.

Since I cannot call the Dalai Lama Your Holiness, what do I say? I call him "my dear friend." What a privilege it is to be able to use those words when addressing this most extraordinary man.

CHAPTER 25

The Paul Ekman Group LLC (PEG)

DURING THIS SAME PERIOD when I was getting to know the Dalai Lama, I had retired from the University, and without making a carefully considered decision I started to develop online training tools and opened a startup company, the Paul Ekman Group LLC (PEG), to market those tools. Sometimes I think it was a mistake, for I had no experience running a small company and I took many missteps. It is not what I like to do, not what I developed my specialized expertise to do, but it did enable me to translate some of my research findings into tools people could use to improve their emotional life. After having forty years of support from the government, I felt an obligation to translate at least some of my work into what could be used to improve people's lives.

The mission statement of PEG states:

MISSION

The Paul Ekman Group seeks to enhance emotional awareness. Building on decades of research, we offer resources to build competency in evaluating truthfulness, improving emotional life and compassionate connection. PEG provides training which facilitates effective communication in professional and personal relationships.

OUR GUIDING PRINCIPLES

- We believe that effective communication skills are the most important skills in life.

- Our training is evidence-based, leavened by real-life experience. We err on the side of under- rather than over-representing the benefits.

- We seek to maximize usage of our trainings and workshops rather than focusing solely on maximizing profit. We undertake relevant pro bono work. Our training tools are made available to accredited researchers at no cost on a case-by-case basis.

- We believe research should have practical application. We offer our training to:

  - National Security and law enforcement

  - Health and social welfare institutions

  - Educational settings

- Corporate settings

- The general public, families, students, and researchers

- We will never conduct evaluations of individuals running for or currently in public office, or in litigation.

HISTORY

Dr. Paul Ekman founded the Paul Ekman Group (PEG) when he retired from University of California, San Francisco, where he was a professor for nearly forty years. He wanted to translate his research findings into practical tools that would equip anyone to lead a more skillful emotional life, and to enable those in law enforcement to more accurately evaluate truthfulness. His emotional skills training tools have been used by governments, security organizations, teachers, therapists, physicians, salespeople, nurses, doctors, and corporate executives all over the world. Ekman has personally conducted workshops for the FBI, the CIA, the U.S. Department of Defense, the Counter-Intelligence School, and the New York Police Department. PEG provides a range of quality-assured Paul Ekman Workshops through Paul Ekman International (PEI) and its network of Licensed Delivery Centers around the globe, making his work more accessible to businesses and individuals. PEG continues to develop online interactive training tools; RETT (Responding Effectively Training Tool) and CAP (Charting your Anger Profile) will be available soon.

I have developed two suites of tools: the face suite and the responding to emotion suite. After a number of approximations I learned what it takes to develop an effective online training tool dealing with faces and emotions. The tools are priced low enough to generate sales easily managed by most people—about the cost of dinner and a movie. We provide the tools to law enforcement and national security *pro bono* if they can't afford the purchase price, but they usually can. We also provide the tools at no cost to researchers, as I want research to determine their benefits. To date, the face suite tools have been shown, by investigators who had no financial stake in the tools, to enhance lie detection, increase the efficacy of salespersons, and to benefit schizophrenia. There are many more studies and endorsements that can be found on my website (www.paulekman.com).

A second set of tools with the awkward name Responding Effectively Training Tool (RETT) provides training in an important set of skills not previously available. RETT deals with family, work, and criminal justice scenarios. The framework can be applied to other situations—for example, a doctor-patient scenario. A third set of tools aimed at couples provides them with an opportunity to see if their perceptions of each other are in line with their self-perceptions. It will be available before this account is published. PEG also participates in classroom training on evaluating truthfulness and emotional skills, through a sister company, Paul Ekman International. My daughter, Eve, the young pretty doctor Ekman, now on a postdoctoral fellowship at UCSF, continues to train people in the Cultivating Emotional Balance course. Eve also has developed her own training program dealing with stress and burnout, which she is applying to health professionals.

My main activity for the last two years was the development of an Atlas of Emotions. Once again, the idea was suggested to me, not mine to begin with. A few years ago the Dalai Lama said that when we wanted to get to the new world we needed a map to get there. Now, he said, we need a map of the emotions to get to a calm state. He further stipulated that such a map should be guided by what science knows about the emotions. A tall order, which I ignored for more than a year, but after hearing reports that he kept talking about the need for such a map I decided to take it on. It was my main focus for the last two years and in mid-2016 became available online at www.atlasofemotions.com.

The first step was to find out what scientists who study emotion agree about, for I could not rely upon my hunch or hopes, or be influenced by those who tried to rattle me with public denunciations of my findings on universality. I decided to focus just on those researchers who use quantitative methods to study emotion, leaving out the qualitative types who inhabit the clinical world, philosophy and anthropology. My justification was that when the Dalai Lama asked that the map be scientifically grounded, he had experimental or at least quantitative science, not the qualitative people, in mind.

A mail survey had a 60 percent return rate and revealed very high agreement about the evidence for universals in some facial expressions. There was very high agreement that the evidence was strong for the existence of just five emotions: anger, fear, sadness, disgust, and enjoyment. Those are the five that the Emotions Atlas deals with, and by coincidence they are the five emotions that Pixar's film *Inside Out* includes, although when I advised Pixar about emotion I emphasized the seven emotions I have been studying, and I had not yet conducted the survey. "What Scientists Who Study Emotion Agree About,"[41] published in January 2016, I expect is the last research study I will conduct.

We are calling it an *Atlas of Emotions*, for an atlas is a group of maps, and we created five maps for users to navigate. The creation of the Atlas was funded by the Dalai Lama trust, with the majority of the money going to the mapping firm, Stamen, that created the maps guided by me and my daughter, Eve. Working with Eric Rodenbeck, the head of Stamen, and one of his designers, Nicolette Hayes, has been both mind stretching and very enjoyable, as they raised issues necessary to create maps that I had not previously thought much about. When we showed our progress to date to the Dalai Lama, he gave no feedback, which was both a surprise and a disappointment. His attitude was that if I think it is correct that is all he needs to know. Although I appreciated his trust in me, I would have preferred not to have so much responsibility. It has led me to think anew about the unanticipated downside of being trusted.

Looking back on my career—a Ph.D. in 1958, fifty-eight years ago!—one of the critical factors in why I enjoyed myself so much, was able to make a few discoveries, and become well known was the lucky coincidence of the younger generation of colleagues and students who worked with me. Having my faculty appointment at UCSF where there was no department of psychology freed me from the major teaching and administrative responsibilities that I would have had if I had been in a psychology department, but it deprived me of graduate students. Only five people got their Ph.D.'s doing dissertations with me; two of them went on to become deans of schools of nursing, and none of them obtained a permanent academic post in psychology. But, I had three exceptional collaborators who became close friends, a generation or two younger than me: Richie Davidson, Bob Levenson, and Klaus Scherer. All three still play a role in my life through friendship, and provide too infrequent intense intellectual discussions. I had a few postdoctoral fellows who I became close to, intellectually and in friendship: Dacher Keltner was the most prominent. Dacher not only developed a very active research program that has substantially expanded on our knowledge of emotions, but he created a center named The Greater Good, which is a beehive of activity focusing on just what its name implies.

A number of the graduates of the postdoctoral training program in emotion have become welcome colleagues; closest by are Jeanne Tsai and Brian Knutson at Stanford. Erika Rosenberg was the last graduate student who did her dissertation with me; an exceptional study I believe. She has carved out an unconventional career on the periphery of the academic world, teaching and looking after the FACS legacy.

Thirty years ago when there was an opportunity for a full professorship in psychology at either UC Berkeley or Stanford, I asked Dick Lazarus at Berkeley and Jerry Kagan at Harvard, both very prominent professors then, how many students had they trained whose subsequent career they felt proud of. Both said about five. I thought I would do so as well where I was, without all the academic burdens, and I didn't seek those positions. I think it was the right choice.

Often when I meet people they say how honored they are to meet me. These are not just students. I have come to be more widely known for some scientific accomplishments, perhaps universals, or spotting liars. I am uncomfortable with such public recognition, because I don't think I belong in the class of people who it should be an honor to meet, but so be it. Becoming a bit known does allow me to sometimes get a comment on a public issue published in a national media outlet and I now have my own platform on the *Huffington Post*. I am interviewed often by print and electronic media, usually about deception and sometimes about emotion. I try very hard to keep to the evidence and not to use my expertise on the topics I have studied to give undeserved weight to my opinions about matters about which I have no expertise.

I have had a great life—wonderful marriage, extraordinary children, and satisfaction, not frustration, with work. Is this despite or because of a terrible childhood and adolescence, in which I was subject to physical abuse, emotional trauma, and years of isolation from other children? Sometimes people ask me how I did it. I answer, "What was the choice?" I never expected to not overcome obstacles.

Shortly before I retired from UCSF in 2000 I was asked to talk to the medical students about what had shaped my scientific career. I entitled the talk "Serendipity,

Perseverance, Aim, and Timing," explaining that these four factors, in order of importance, were responsible for my success. If any one of them had been missing I would have failed. Upon reflection I recognize that most of the discoveries I made in fifty years of research were the result of accidents (the creation of the Facial Action Coding System, FACS, and the taxonomy of hand movements are the exceptions). I didn't sit down and think through what was the logical, next step of research that needed to be done. Most of the time I didn't recognize what question was begging for an answer. Instead a question fell into my lap, and when it did I picked it up, recognized its importance, and ran with it as hard as I could to resolve it. I was lucky. Many people helped me along the way. And the time was ripe to make discoveries about a topic, facial expressions, that has relevance to so many different aspects of life, and fascinates experts and a more general public. It has been a wonderful life!

August 2016

Endnotes

1. Lim S.L., et al. (2015) "Correction: HENMT1 and piRNA Stability Are Required for Adult Male Germ Cell Transposon Repression and to Define the Spermatogenic Program in the Mouse." *PLoS Genetics* 11(12): e1005782. doi: 10.1371/journal.pgen.1005782

2. Arieti, S. (1955). *Interpretation of Schizophrenia*. R. Brunner.

3. Ekman, P. (1957). "A Methodological Discussion of Nonverbal Behavior." *The Journal of Psychology*, 43, 141–149.

4. Ekman, P., Friesen, W. V., & Ellsworth, P. (1972). *Emotion in the Human Face: Guidelines for Research and an Integration of Findings*. Elmsford, NY: Pergamon Press Inc.

5. Ekman, P. (1965). "Communication through Nonverbal Behavior: A Source of Information about an Interpersonal Relationship." In Tomkins, S. S. & Izard, C. E. (Eds.), *Affect, Cognition and Personality: Empirical Studies* (pp. 390–442). Oxford, England: Springer.

6. Ekman, P. & Friesen, W. V. (1967). "Head and Body Cues in the Judgement of Emotion: A Reformulation." *Perceptual and Motor Skills*, 24, 711–724.

7. Efron, D. (1941). *Gesture and Environment*. New York: King's Crown Press. Reissued as: *Gesture, Environment, and Culture*. The Hague: Mouton Press, 1972.

8. Ekman, P. (editor) (2003). *Emotions Inside Out: 130 Years after Darwin's* The Expression of the Emotions in Man and Animals (1st ed.), New York: New York Academy of Sciences.

9. Ekman, P. & Friesen W. V. (1972). "Hand Movements." *Journal of Communication*, 22, 353–374.

10. Johnson, H. G., Ekman, P., & Friesen, W. V. (1975). "Communicative Body Movements: American Emblems." *Semiotica*, 15(4), 335–353.

11. Ekman, P. (1976). "Movements with Precise Meanings." *Journal of Communication*, 26(3), 14–26.

12. Verplanck, W.S. (1955) "The Operant, from Rat to Man: An Introduction to Some Recent Experiments on Human Behavior." *Transactions, The New York Academy of Sciences* 17 Ser. II, 594–601.

13. Ekman, P., Cohen, L., Moos, R., Raine, W., Schlesinger, M., & Stone, G. (1963). "Divergent Reactions to the Threat of War." *Science*, 139, 88–94.

14. Ekman, P., Tufte, E. R., Archibald, K., & Brody, R. A. (1966). "Coping with Cuba-Divergent Policy Preferences of State Political Leaders." *Journal of Conflict Resolution*, 10, 180–197.

15. Verba, S., Brody, R. A., Parker, E. B., Nie, N.H., Polsby, N. W., Ekman, P. & Black. G. S. (1967). "Public Opinion and the War in Vietnam." *American Political Science Review*, 61, 317–333. doi:10.2307/1953248.

16. Ekman, P., Friesen, W. V., & Ellsworth, P. (1972). Emotion in the Human Face: Guidelines for Research and an Integration of Findings. Elmsford, NY: Pergamon Press Inc.

17. Ekman, P., Friesen, W. V., O'Sullivan, M., Chan, A., Diacoyanni-Tarlatzis, I., Heider, K., . . . Tzavaras, A. (1987). "Universals and Cultural Differences in the Judgment of Facial Expressions of Emotion." *Journal of Personality and Social Psychology*, 53(4), 712–717.

18. Ekman, P. (1972). "Universals and Cultural Differences in Facial Expressions of Emotions." In Cole, J. (Ed.), *Nebraska Symposium on Motivation* (pp. 207–282). Lincoln, NB: University of Nebraska Press.

19. Ekman, P. (ed.) (2009). *The Expression of the Emotions in Man and Animals.* (by Charles Darwin), Anniversary edition. London: Harper.

20. Ibid.

21. For example, instead of asking what is happening when you observe someone with their brows raised and eyes widened, he gave the answer in his question: "Is astonishment expressed by the eyes and mouth being opened wide, and by the eyebrows being raised?" He did

note the importance of obtaining answers to this and fifteen other questions by people who had observed ". . . natives who have had little communication with Europeans . . ."

22. Ekman, P., Friesen, W. V., & Taussig, T. G. (1969). "VID-R and SCAN: Tools and Methods for the Automated Analysis of Visual Records." In Gerbner, G., Holsti, O., Krippendorff, K., Paisley, W., & Stone, P. (Eds.), *The Analysis of Communication Content* (pp. 297–312). New York: Wiley & Sons.

23. Ekman, P. & Friesen, W. V. (1969). "The Repertoire of Nonverbal Behavior: Categories, Origins, Usage, and Coding." *Semiotica*, 1 (1), 49–98.

24. Ekman, P. & Friesen, W. V. (1969). "Nonverbal Leakage and Clues to Deception." *Psychiatry*, 32(1), 88–106.

25. Ekman, P., Friesen, W. V., & Tomkins, S. S. (1971). "Facial Affect Scoring Technique: A First Validity Study." *Semiotica*, 3, 37–58.

26. Duchenne (de Boulogne), G. B. 1876. Mécanisme de la physionomie humaine ou analyse électro-physiologique de l'expression des passions. Texte: Première partie. Deuxième édition. Paris: Librairie J. B. Bailliere et Fils.

27. Cuthbertson, R. A. (Ed. and Transl.) (2006). *The Mechanism of Human Facial Expression* (pp. 270–284). Cambridge: Cambridge University Press.

28. Hjortsjö, C. H. (1969). *Man's Face and Mimic Language*. Lund: Sweden: Studentlitteratur.

29. Ekman, P. & Friesen, W. V. (1978) *Facial Action Coding System: A Technique for the Measurement of Facial Movement*. Palo Alto, CA: Consulting Psychologists Press.

30. Ekman, P., & Rosenberg, E. L. (1997). What the Face Reveals: Basic and Applied Studies of Spontaneous Expression Using the Facial Action Coding System (FACS). New York: Oxford University Press.

31. Ekman, P. (1985). *Telling Lies*. New York: W. W. Norton & Company, Inc.

32. Ekman, P. (2003). *Emotions Revealed*. New York: Henry Holt.

33. Ekman, P. & O'Sullivan, M. (1991). "Who Can Catch a Liar?." *American Psychologist*, 46(9), 913–920.

34. Ekman, P., O'Sullivan, M., & Frank, M. G. (1999). "A Few Can Catch a Liar." *Psychological Science,* 10(3), 263–266.

35. Anderson, C. A., Berkowitz, L., Donnerstein, E., Huesmann, R. L., Johnson, J. D., Linz, D., Malamuth, N. M. Wartella, E. (2003). "The Influence of Media Violence on Youth." *Psychological Science in the Public Interest,* 4(3), 81–110.

36. *Floating in the Air, Followed by the Wind: Thaipusam, a Hindu Festival.* Produced and Directed by Ronald C. Simons; Photography by Gunter Pfaff. 16mm film. 34 minutes. Color, Optical sound. (Distributed by Indiana University Audio-Visual Center).

37. A few years earlier Haggard and Isaacs described having seen what they called "micromomentary expressions." They thought these expressions are not detectable without slow-motion viewing. We know that is not so, that some people can detect them at real time. They also said micro expressions are the result of repression, revealing information about which the person is unaware. We have no reason to doubt that does occur, and in a few clinical case studies we found support for their contention, but micro expressions also occur with deliberate concealment.

38. Ekman, P. & Friesen, W. V. (1969). "Nonverbal Leakage and Clues to Deception." *Psychiatry,* 32(1), 88–106.

39. Ekman, P., (2003). "Darwin, Deception, and Facial Expression." In Ekman, P., Campos, J. J., Davidson, R. J., & de Waal, F. B. M. (Eds.), *Emotions Inside Out: 130 Years after Darwin's* The Expression of the Emotions in Man and Animals (pp. 205–221). New York: New York Academy of Sciences.

40. Kemeny, M. E., et al. (2012). "Contemplative/Emotion Training Reduces NegaEmotional Behavior and Promotes Prosocial Responses." *Emotion,* 2012 Apr; 12(2), 338–350. PMID: 22148989.

41. Ekman, P. (2016). "What Scientists Who Study Emotion Agree About." *Perspectives on Psychological Science,* 11(1), 31–34.

Index

gestural slips, 9–10. *See also* bodily movements
Gingrich, Newt, 226
Glaser, Don, 107
Goffman, Erving, 79, 96
Goldsmith, Sadja, 51
Goleman, Dan, 174, 246, 248, 263,
good fortune, 41
Good Morning America, 193
Gorbachev, 122, 134
Gorman, Frank, 269
Goroka, 57–58
Gottman, John, 172
grant proposals, writing, 190–191
Grazier, Brian, 193–194
The Greater Good, 279
Greenberg, Mark, 247, 249, 262
Guggenheim foundation, 103–104
Gulag, 122
"guru of kuru," 53
Gwyne Jones, Philip, 84

H

hair, cultural differences in, 203
Hall, Edward T., 47
Han Chinese immigrants, 245–246
hand movements, interpreting, 37–38
happiness, 48
    cross-cultural context, 70
    expressing, 76
hard labor versus stockade, 18
"hard money," 226
Harman, Sabrina, 216–221
Harper Collins London, 84
Harrington, Anne, 249
Harris, Robert E., 20, 25
Harrison, Randy, 202–203
Harvard, visit to, 89
hatred, end of, 255
Hayes, Nicolette, 278
Heider, Karl, 70–71, 77, 175–176
Herron, Jeannine, 167
Hersh, Seymour, 223
HHDL (His Holiness the Dalai Lama), 270. *See also* Dalai Lama
Highland peoples, 57
His Holiness. *See* Dalai Lama

Hjortsjö, Carl-Herman, 102, 153
Hoffman, Neville, 59–60, 69, 74
Holy Mother, reported discussions with, 167–168
horror, 221
horses in the race, 110
hospitalization, of patients with severe depression, 35
Huffington Post, 280
Human Interaction and Conflict, 92
Humphries, 34
"hyper-startlers," 182. *See also Startle Responses*

I

Identity recognition, 106
illustrator classification, 37, 95
imprinting, 212
Improvement Measure, 240
Industrial Light and Magic, 105
injury, anticipation of, 58
Inside Out, 272
intellectual-spiritual fads, 245
intent, considering, 24
International Department, 125
interviews with patients, filming, 35
"Invictus," 41
IPAR (Institute of Personality and Research), 26–27
IRB (Institutional Review Board), 138
Islam, 264
Israeli National Police, 110
Izard, Carol, 49–50

J

Jackson, Don, 22
Japan
    Ainu of, 181
    completing, 78
    trip to, 73
Japanese subjects, 49
    facial expressions of, 74
    facial movements, 97
    films shown to, 72
Jinpa, Thupten, 253–254, 260, 265–266
Johnny Carson Show, 193

Index   291

psychiatric assessments, timing of, 20
psychiatry versus emotions, 163–164
psychology, founding of field of, 83
psychotic episodes, 19
"Public Opinion and the War in Vietnam," 30
purchasing, change in, 232–233

Q

Quakers, 51
questions, addressing, 20

R

race and sex bias research project, 202–203
racism, challenging, 82
RETT (Responding Effectively Training Tool), 241–242, 275–276
religious beliefs, differences in, 264
"The Repertoire of Nonverbal Behavior," 95
research
  benefit of, 18–19
  following path of, 19–20
research institutes, attempts at creating, 211–213
research projects
  emotional profiles, 209–211
  facial muscular tension and expression, 205–207
  friendship, 202
  genes and facial expressions, 207–209
  practical application, 268
  race and sex bias, 202–203
  subjective emotional experience, 203–205
  unpublished, 201
retirement
  postponement, 234
  from UCSF, 275
Ricard, Matthieu, 247–248, 253, 259
Rodenbeck, Eric, 278
Rosch, Eleanor, 77
Rosenberg, Erika, 105, 195, 279
Rosenthal, Abe, 135
Roth, Tim, 195, 199

Ruesch, Jurgen, 14
rules. *See* display rules
Russia, Olympics in, 122
Ryan, Leo, 32
Rynearson, Robert, 36–37

S

sad and fear repetitions, 36
sadness, 48, 70, 76, 204
Sakharov, 122, 132
salaries, paying, 229–230
San Francisco State College, teaching at, 27
Sanford, Nevitt, 26
Sarlo, George, 224
Saron, Cliff, 207, 259
satisfaction, finding, 250
scale system, 203–204
Scherer, Klaus, 212, 279
schizophrenics, 234
Schneider, Stan, 159–160
schoolboys, 65, 67
Schransky, 122, 132
Schwartz, Gary, 206
Science, 174, 187
scientific accomplishments
  accuracy of nonverbal behaviors, 7
  detection of lies, 119
  FACS (Facial Action Coding System), 105
  gestural slips, 9
  universality of facial expressions, 78
  voluntary facial expressions, 177
Seaford, Wade, 97
Sebeok, Tom, 95
Secret Service, 119, 198
Sejnowski, Terry, 107–108
Sejnowski-Bartlett team, 110
"self-adaptors," 38
self-adaptors, 95
Semantic Differential, 47
Semiotica, 95
sentences, reading, 75
"Serendipity, Perseverance, Aim, and Timing," 280–281

If you'd like to learn more about Dr. Ekman, his research, his work with the Dalai Lama and media, and the online training tools he has created, visit www.paulekman.com.

Printed in Great Britain
by Amazon